SELECTED WRITINGS OF

JUAN RAMÓN JIMÉNEZ

TRANSLATED BY H. R. HAYS

EDITED WITH A PREFACE BY EUGENIO FLORIT

FARRAR, STRAUS AND GIROUX

NEW YORK

Copyright © 1957 by Juan Ramón Jiménez
The lectures on "Aristocracy and Democracy" and
"Poetry and Literature" have appeared in Spanish
in the University of Miami Hispanic-American
Studies, No. 2, 1941. The poems "Convalescence,"
"Francina in the Garden," "Morning of the Cross"
and "New Spring" appeared in Mademoiselle
magazine. The poem "The Little Green Girl"
appeared in Partisan Review magazine.
Library of Congress catalog card number 57-12158
First Printing, 1957
Published simultaneously in Canada by
Ambassador Books, Ltd., Toronto. Manufactured
in the United States by H. Wolff, New York
Design: Marshall Lee
ISBN 0-374-52745-8

CONTENTS

3 *1916-1925/A new approach to poetry and prose*

4 *1925-1936/From the years of maturity in rhythm and thought*

5 *1940/Portraits of writers and artists*

6 *1941/Ideas on society and poetry*

7 *1936-1956/From the latest books written in America*

PREFACE

In the last decades of the nineteenth century a literary movement appeared that, originating in Spanish America, was to spread swiftly across the Atlantic and through Spain to modify and change the complete picture of its poetry. I refer to modernism. The genius and personal influence of the Nicaraguan poet, Rubén Darío (1867-1916), was principally responsible for this. He and his followers conducted their poetry through two main parallel and in many instances concurrent ways: one, of Parnassian origin, concerned above all with form and the exterior appearance of the poem together with some interest in exotic or decadent themes or subjects, and the other akin to symbolism or to more traditional trends, but closer to the innermost and secret anxieties of the human soul.

Paralleling the influence and skill of Rubén Darío other factors contributed to the creation of the contemporary spirit in Spain, namely the one known to us in literary history by the name of "generación del 98" which we cannot separate from the modernist movement because most writers in those years held on to and partook of the traits of both sides. These traits were confined, on the one hand, to a deep preoccupation in "discovering" the essence of Spanish character by searching into its history and its soul, and on the other hand in attempting to overcome the political disaster in which the war with the United States had ended. Among the former another great figure appears, Miguel de Unamuno (1864-1937), a stubborn non-conformist with reality and its circumstances, more intensely concerned than any one of his contemporaries with the revival of the Spanish spirit. This phase, a key to Spain and its literature, oscillated between two points (sometimes coincident in the same author), one that could be called the "agonic" mood, to use the word so dear to the professor of Salamanca, with emphasis on the transcendental in thought, history and time; and the other one of emphasis on formal expression in poetry, combined with the melancholy accent which for a time seemed to characterize the group of the modernists.

These were days of novelty, of experimentation with new forms or with old ones re-evaluated by the Spanish American poets; a world of restlessness in which the Spanish writers wished to inform themselves of the latest in literature, establish contacts with the outside world, be "modern," express a particular form of escapism allied with a timeless lyricism. It is interesting to observe that the great literary revolutions in Spain, petrarchism and romanticism, had their birth in the desire to widen the cultural and geographical limits of the country, to accept, adapt and incorporate in literature, especially in poetry, other great movements of the European spirit without negating the national characteristics which continue living along with the rest. This process is particularly evident in modernism.

In this atmosphere the poetry of Juan Ramón Jiménez began to develop. From his birthplace at Moguer he started sending poems to the newspapers in Seville and they were not only accepted but quickly praised, so much so that he was soon recognized and well-received among the men of letters of the capital city. The magazine *Vida Nueva* of Madrid published his verses. His friends invited him to join them in the literary revolution. It was actually Rubén Darío who with Francisco Villaespesa signed the letter of invitation. Thus, in April, 1900, eighteen year old Juan Ramón, a young Andalusian poet, arrived in Madrid to take part in the literary Spanish life from which he would never separate himself.

During that year he published his two first books, *Almas de violeta* and *Ninfeas,* both exceptionally well-received by the élite but with indignation on the part of some of the critics who, as is always the case everywhere, react violently against innovations. The delicate health of the poet became apparent following the death of his father, and in 1901 he was forced to spend several months at a sanatorium in Bordeaux, in the south of France, and later at one in Madrid. In spite of this, it was a period of great activity in his life. In 1902 he published several books and founded with some friends the magazine *Helios,* one of the culminating landmarks in the revolution of modernism in Spain. This was followed, in 1907, by the appearance of *Renacimiento,* the review representing the triumph of the movement. Both enterprises enjoyed the close collaboration of Spanish American and Spanish writers. This collaboration aided in establishing better relationships between Spain and Spanish America, uniting them in a spiritual communion of ideals and a common cultural destiny.

After the publication of his first important book, *Arias tristes*

(1903), there followed his *Jardines lejanos* (1904) and *Pastorales* (1905). Then Juan Ramón, having supervised the editing of Darío's book, *Cantos de vida y esperanza,* while the Nicaraguan poet was in Paris in 1905, returned to Moguer where he remained in contact with his people and landscape until 1912. During this period were published *Olvidanzas, Baladas de primavera* and several other books of poems. He worked as well on the manuscript of *Platero y yo,* not to be published until years later, in 1917. This was the period of Jiménez's greatest formal elaboration of his poetry, as shown in *Elejías* (1908), *Poemas májicos y dolientes* (1909) and *Laberinto* (1911).

The year 1916 stands out as crucial in the life and work of the poet. In that year he made his first trip to the United States to marry Zenobia Camprubí who, after their engagement in Madrid, had come to New York to visit with her relatives. The trip, the wedding and the return of the young couple to Spain are recorded in one of the most important of Juan Ramón's books, the *Diario de un poeta recien casado,* published in 1917. This book is not only of consequence in the sum of the poet's work but also in the history of contemporary Spanish poetry. In the same year several more books of poetry appeared, such as *Estío* and *Sonetos espirituales:* they represent the end of a period in Jiménez's work, as the *Diario* inaugurated the beginning of a new one.

Juan Ramón Jiménez spent the following years in Madrid, collaborating with his wife on literary tasks, such as the translations of the complete works of the Hindu poet Rabindranath Tagore, advising the young poets who were always about him, publishing magazines and short articles, and working in the editing and revision of his own work to which he was constantly striving to impart unity. In 1922 his *Segunda antolojía poética* (1898-1918) was published, a volume that is fundamental for the study of his poetry up to that period. A previous anthology,

Poesías escojidas (1899-1917) had been sponsored by the Hispanic Society of America in New York and published in Madrid in 1917 in a handsome edition of 600 copies signed by the author and not destined for sale—in fact, it was not distributed at all—and it is a bibliographical rarity.

In 1936 still another important work appeared, *Canción*, a collection of poems alike in mood and form. This was part of Jiménez's project to bring together *Romance, Estancia, Arte menor, Silva* and other books of prose, all of which would present under the general title of *Unidad* the totality of his literary production from 1895 on. The Spanish Civil War, however, interrupted this phase of his life and he made his second trip to America. During 1936 and 1937 he and his wife lived in Puerto Rico and Cuba, dedicated to his literary work, serving as an inspiration to the young poets who gathered about him and received his advice. Then he came to the United States to live successively in New York, Washington, D.C., and Coral Gables in Florida, always supported by the assiduous understanding and devotion of his wife. Jiménez's health, which was never good, forced him into hospitals from time to time, and at other times he would seclude himself in his home. Nevertheless he continued to work on the organization of his manuscripts and projected books. At last, because of his health and because of a natural nostalgia for all that is Hispanic, including, above all, his mother tongue, he returned to Puerto Rico in 1952 to teach at the university. He continued to enjoy periods of relative good health followed by periods of depression and melancholy from which he has suffered since his youth. In November 1956 two dramatically opposed events overtook him: the news of the award of the Nobel Prize for Literature and the death three days later of his wife, his faithful companion and collaborator throughout forty years. She was a noble example of heroism, kindness and love.

xviii

2

Juan Ramón Jiménez once said: "Without a doubt contemporary Spanish poetry begins with Bécquer." Bécquer is the nexus, the union with symbolism, and his poetry was influential in Spanish America as well as in Spain by the end of the last century. Along with Bécquer, the influence of the French symbolists and of Edgar Allen Poe appear. Jiménez was, therefore, born to poetry under the sign of a poet whose delicacy, vagueness and musical idiom are perfectly in accord with the restlessness of Jiménez's soul. Juan Ramón also read and absorbed Verlaine and Samain, some of the German poets (Goethe, Holderlin), the English (Shakespeare, Keats, Shelley, Browning), the Italians (Dante, Petrarch, Carducci, D'Annunzio) without neglecting his own Spanish poets such as St. John of the Cross, the Romancero, Espronceda, the more modern Verdaguer, Curros Enriquez (whose Galician poems he translated), Rosalía Castro. But of course and above all, Bécquer.

Bécquer's influence is noticeable at the beginning of Jiménez's work even to the name given to the book, *Rimas* (1902), almost all of which was written in Bordeaux. According to Jiménez's own statement this volume showed a reaction to modernism, marking a return to Bécquer from whom he had temporarily severed himself when he followed the fashion of Darío and the modernists. It is likewise true that Darío's *Rimas* in 1887 were proof of the Master's admiration and reading of the Sevillian poet. We find in Juan Ramón all these elements, Bécquer plus symbolism plus Rubén Darío with certain tones or undertones of some of the other modernist poets, Silva for example. Later on, after the delicate simplicity of such early books as *Baladas de primavera, Jardines lejanos* and the series of his pastoral themes, an evolving force began in the poet about 1907 toward more formal rhetoric with the reiterated use of the alexandrine, the fourteen syllable line of modernism. If there exists a "modernist" verse form line, it is the alexandrine used by all the poets of that period. Here we may refer to the innovation of Garcilaso de la Vega in the first half of the sixteenth century in the sense that as in our Renaissance it is the hendecasyllable of Italian origin which establishes itself prominently in Spanish poetry as it later does in French, English and elsewhere, so it is the alexandrine in modernism. The difference is, though, that the latter was not totally foreign, since a great deal of Spanish thirteenth and fourteenth century poetry—in fact all of our important *mester de clerecía*—are written in these forms, from the time of Berceo until don Pedro López de Ayala. The alexandrine, then, was not new in Spanish poetry. What the modernists did was to adapt some of the French accentuation, and to clothe it in rich imagery, giving it exotic color and subtle cadences, which could already be observed in some of the magnificent verses of la Avellaneda, Zorrilla, Mármol and many of the romantics. It is this modernist alexandrine that operates with great importance in a part of Jiménez's work and is present in the *Elejías* (1907-1908) and in the major part of his books of poetry written between 1907 and 1913.

With the appearance of *La frente pensativa* (1911-1912) there is a noticeable reluctance on the part of Jiménez to use the ornamental style, and a return toward a freer poetic expression, what he calls "naked poetry." The regular strophic structure, also the regularity of verse, syllabically accentuated—I do not refer to the eight and nine syllable measure or other forms of versification more in keeping with popular or traditional currents, but to the one we shall call "culta"—appears later on in Jiménez, and especially in a book, *Sonetos espirituales* (1914-1915) which as I have said represents the end of an epoch and style in his poetry. He recalls, regarding this, that during the seven years he spent in Moguer, between 1905 and 1912, he devoted himself to reading the Spanish classical writers—"I nourished myself with their work," he says—and the fusing of all the "freedom of life and reading" determined a style that would culminate and end in the *Sonetos espirituales*. When he returned to Madrid in 1912 he worked on the sonnets, wrote *Estío* and also completed the editing of *Platero y yo*. The sonnets we are now referring to are not in the modernistic alexandrine in which so many poems of this type were written in those days in our language, but instead they use the classical hendecasyllable line of the Golden Age though expressed within a modernist tonality and lyricism.

Estío (1913-1915) published in 1917, reveals a more pronounced refinement of the essential elements of poetry, pointing to a marked preference for a free style without forgetting—for they are ever present in Jiménez—the octosyllabic verse. And this freedom, resulting each time in a more original expression of his personality, was developed further and acquired a greater importance in the *Diario de un poeta recien casado*, written in 1916 and published the following year. In this book, it seems to me, we can see more clearly the contemporaneousness of the poet, his originality, the daring of his imagery, his art of translating in a literary fashion spirit, sensations and emotions of all sorts. Here one feels, above all, the sea; that sea crossed and meditated upon by the poet and commented on in a thousand ways as diverse as its waves and colors. Here, too, is the landscape of a new country, the United States, with New York, Boston, Flushing, seen through the sensibility of a Spanish European poet in brief, impressionistic word pictures. And also, even more than in *Platero y yo* appears the novelty of an agile, nervous prose, illuminated by unusual images like the luminous advertisements in Times Square, images that point toward a horizon in Spain for the "avant garde," the poetical schools of the first postwar period. One has only to read some of the impressions of Times Square, of the subways, of the cemeteries, the people and atmosphere of the "America del nordeste" to understand how much the poetry of the Spanish language owes to this crucial book, which is, as the author has said, the first in a new period in his work; the one which has had such beneficial influence on Spanish and Spanish American poets; and which he confesses is his best because "it was given to me united by love, the great sea, the distant sky, free verse, the Americas and my former long periods of work." The earlier work should not be forgotten, though, since what Jiménez does in the *Diario* is to polish to its ultimate degree, to perfect the originality that had never been absent from his former books.

Eternidades belongs to that same period (1916-1917) and it shows a preoccupation that can be called "intellectual"—*Inteligencia, dame/el nombre exacto de las cosas* (Intelligence, give me/the exact name of things)—which nevertheless does not obscure the simple strain of its octosyllabic verse, rooted in the traditional and popular. In this book we find the well-known poem—a sort of history of his poetic life—which begins, *Vino, primero, pura,/vestida de inocencia* (She came, at first, pure/ dressed in innocence), and goes on to tell how his verse as time passed was clothed with *no sé qué ropajes* (I know not what clothing) to return later to its initial innocence until it reached "total nakedness." This poem seems to be a developed version, perfected and elaborated to its ultimate possibilities, of a poem by W. B. Yeats appearing in his book *Responsibilities* (1914) with the title of *A Coat.* Yeats's poem is made up of ten lines as contrasted with eighteen of Jiménez's, and even though the idea in the Spanish poem seems more ample and carried to a greater realization, the similarity in essence does not seem too farfetched. This of course may be no more than a coincidence as so often happens in literature. We do know that Jiménez read the English poets and especially Yeats, some of whose works he has translated. It is curious that a brief poem by the Irish writer, and one that does not seem to be of great importance within the full scope of his poetry, has been converted by the Spanish writer into a beautiful and important piece. Also it is interesting to observe how they coincide in the process of self-criticism and self-examination of their own work.

In *Piedra y cielo* (1917-1918) Jiménez continues to purify, to discover the one essential line in the poem, as demonstrated by *No le toques ya más,/que así es la rosa.* (Do not touch it any more/thus is the rose.) In its essence this poem results in an esthetic program about which much could be said since it does not seem to be in accord with the constant retouching, rewriting or changing that Jiménez has done on his work. To what extreme is the *ya más* (no more) the end? Or better still, when do we arrive at that *ya más*? Undoubtedly for the poet that moment is hardly a point in time, if we are to consider his concept of the atemporal character of his work, constantly evolving and yet never complete. Then, that point of *ya más* is a hypothetical moment one must continually pursue in order to reach, as the rose transforms itself from seed to stem to branchlet and bud and lastly from bud to the completed flower.

Two more books of poems, *Belleza* and *Poesía* (1917-1923), twins one might say, were published in 1923 and both accentuate the essential part of the poet's work, that becomes more and more subjective and intimate with light accents of intellectualism and a constant meditation on those very words: poetry and beauty. Together, the two offer the key to Jiménez's preoccupation. It is not a question of deciding in his works the relationship between poetry and truth, as in Goethe's case; between beauty and truth as in Keats or Emily Dickinson but between beauty and poetry which with love, woman and death form the abiding themes of his life. Death, for example, is constantly present in the poet of Moguer. He has said, "My three presences: nakedness, work, death." At times the *death* of Rilke is recalled by Jiménez's figure of death. This theme becomes almost an obsession, and it can be seen that this preoccupation with the death of others is nothing other than the mirror of his own imagined death, almost xxiii

a dialogue with it. Now, too, we can appreciate how the total work of the poet of Moguer could be—and in fact is—a triumph, not over the D'Annunzio style of death, but over death itself; the triumph of beauty and of poetry; the ultimate triumph of the permanent over the temporal and perishable.

Canción, published in Madrid in 1936, is a handsome volume in which the author has collected diverse poems united by a rhythmic and almost "sung" tonality, giving at the same time a definite character to it, when considered along with his entire work. This is achieved by the quality of the poems chosen from his earlier work and by some that indicate future themes for future books. With regard to the tone of *Canción,* one can see a certain aspect of the poetry of Jiménez, namely its popular flavor. In the tradition of the great Spanish poets of all times, the kind of poetry that we call "culta" is not the sole factor present in his books. From the beginning to the present, the two currents—"culta" and popular—are entwined and as was true in Lope de Vega and Góngora and always in Spain, both aspects attempt to separate or unite themselves, one superimposing itself over the other, yet never reaching an absolute divorce, since one stems from the other and both are equally important and fundamental. And in Juan Ramón Jiménez the popular trend is the voice of the "copla," with its light burden which from time to time asserts itself, reassuring us of its presence.

Another collection of Jiménez's poems, composed between 1923 and 1936, the year of the beginning of the Spanish Civil War and the poet's second trip to America, was not published until ten years later, in Buenos Aires. This book is *La estación total,* in which Juan Ramón continued with his thought more and more purified, but here his lyrical expression has acquired even broader tonalities of eloquence. Appearing in this book, together with shorter poems, are others that are broader, wider, as if written in a louder voice. This does not mean that the poet has returned to the forms of 1907. No, the form is of the present, the verse freer, sometimes with irregular assonants, sometimes without rhyming. But what promotes the eloquence I see in them is the impetus, the reiterating of words, the interior rhythm which appears more spontaneously. Its romantic climate, if one may call it that, is evident here, as in former periods, but now with greater frankness and freedom, less restriction. An example of this would be the three prose strophes of *Espacio,* the first of which appeared in verse form in 1943. This mood continues in the rest of Jiménez's work up until his last poems, maintaining always an affectionate point of contact with all the simpler and schematic forms appearing here and there in all his books; for instance the ballad form of his *Romances de Coral Gables* published in Mexico in 1948, written between 1939 and 1942 and incorporated in his collection *En el otro costado* (1936-1942) that forms part of the *Tercera antolojía poética* just published. We see, then, that he does not abandon his traditional forms—the *romance* is cultivated by him from his early years as it is found in *Rimas de sombra* (1898-1902), but the difference lies in his awareness that his sensibility during those days was somewhat superficial, with overtones of nostalgia and a symbolist-romantic accent. With the passage of time this has given way to something quite different: the expression, perhaps the clearest one, of the author's pantheism, of his absolute identification with nature, hills, trees, water, birds; a pantheism that could well give the title to all his work as "landscape of a soul," in which the objective reality, that of the senses—to see, hear, smell, touch and taste—seems to live only in the romantic function with the "I," as the transformer, ruler and sum of his circumstances.

Jiménez gives us the emotion of the landscape through the medium of symbols as before; that symbolism absorbed from Verlaine and Samain, reduced to an essential point through contact with the most naked elements of Rubén Darío's verse. Jiménez was able to extract the essential elements of the formal aspect of modernism while conveniently rejecting the glorious.

but transient elements. Rubén Darío has written an immortal line: *De desnuda que está, brilla la estrella* (From its own nakedness the star does shine). And this nakedness, this desire to reach the very essence of a verse has been the constant preoccupation, the target always aimed at by the poet of *Eternidades*. I must repeat that even before the influence of Verlaine, Juan Ramón had already absorbed the musicality and the marvelous want of precision of Bécquer and Rosalia Castro. Thus it can be seen how such a beginning was to produce through the work of grace and devotion, applied will, intelligence and sensibility the most complete expression of what we understand as poetry, a poetry that surpasses fashion and schools, a poetry of his own, in itself. I recall an aphorism of the poet: "When modernism, imagism, or surrealism, for example, produces a great poem (and it has produced, is producing and will continue to produce them), then it ceases to be called surrealism, imagism or modernism and again is called poetry." To this sentence we could add another one: "The classical is, solely, living." In this life of the work, in the perennial struggle to make a living thing of it, that is to say, to make it classical, very few poets have been able to match Juan Ramón Jiménez's efforts. It can be defined as work struggling against temporality, against anecdote. Or again, the struggle against death; surpassing and mastering it because of its integration with the essence of total nature and absolute being.

As in all true creators, the latest poetry of Juan Ramón has risen in tone, in importance, becoming more and more transcendental. The poet begins writing to give an outlet to his feelings, to tell of his impressions of the physical and sentimental circumstances that surround him or that are within him. He tells of that which makes up his life. But that life, when the poet in living it fulfills the eternal, when living is not merely living but transcending life, eternalizing the moment through the medium of the poem, fusing the temporal with the eternal so that this human work of his is poured superhumanly into eternity—

and we note this word "eternity" is always present in the poetry
and prose of our poet so that it almost becomes another of its
principal motifs—that life, I repeat, cannot then fail to produce
anything other than the organization of a total philosophical or
religious system. With Jiménez the constant preoccupation with
beauty as an essential idea has evolved into a religious concept
coinciding with the idea of divinity, of a God "possible through
beauty," in his own words. His last book published in 1949, *Animal de fondo,* included in the *Tercera antolojía poética* with the
more general title of *Dios deseado y deseante* represents the cul-
mination of a process of searching for the religious. He himself
tells us that this appears in three different periods of his life
and work: first, as a sensitive giving of self; then as an intel-
lectual phenomenon; and lastly as a reality, "as a finding of the
true, sufficient and just." It is a god of beauty that is referred to,
a type of religion of the beautiful and poetic, a fact present in
him from the beginning but the revelation of which has not
been solely as poetry or beauty but as a more profound and total
concept; a god summation of interior and exterior moments of
love and adoration. A word which is already an absolute con-
sciousness of the god of his life and work. A metaphysical pre-
occupation, as the poet once said, began for the youth of those
times with the teachings of Miguel de Unamuno, just as "our
own conscious concern with style" began with Rubén Darío; and
from the fusing of these two conditions, those two great differ-
ences, springs the true new poetry. To this end, Jiménez has
arrived by a slow, steady process which makes the sentence from
Goethe chosen by him as his motto very significant: "As the
star, without haste and without rest."

3

Juan Ramón has achieved importance not only by his poetry
but also in a very special manner by his prose. We have already

mentioned *Platero y yo*,* the best known of his prose works, written during the period in which the poet, after a stay in Madrid and France, had returned to his native city of Moguer. The book is a series of lyrical impressions in prose: the author talks to his small donkey, confiding in him his innermost thoughts, his ideas, his feelings. It is thus the discourse of a man. It is "I" plus Platero. But this is not all. The small Platero is always present in those pages chewing on flowers and fresh little leaves, frightening the children or playing with them, moving about the countryside, at one time injuring his foot with a thorn, at another winning a race and a crown of parsley; always tender, enchanting. There is still another quality present. This book is, as the author subtitles it, an "Andalusian elegy." In its pages are to be found the poet, the donkey, and Moguer, a town in southern Andalusia with its surrounding countryside and people. There, immortalized, are the men and women and children in their daily life, eating, moving about, playing and there, too, is silence, the meditation by the well, interrupted by the chatter of the gypsies; and death, too, the death of a small girl and lastly the death of Platero. And one constantly sees the children, running, singing, dancing, playing, those children so loved by the poet, those who in his older days have sat next to him in Puerto Rico and have laughed together. It is the soft breath of daily living, of customs, of landscape, of flowers and sky which comprise, in my opinion, the enchantment of the book. And it is the originality of Jiménez's natural prose, smooth without strident notes, filled with the typical pronunciation of the province of Huelva, where Moguer is located, with a harmonious movement of the hill under the setting sun. *Platero y yo* is Platero and Juan Ramón and the summation of the two with the circumstances, atmosphere, town and countryside. For this reason this is not only a book for children but for adults as well; for all adults who love at times to recall their childhood years.

* Published in a complete translation by the University of Texas Press.

And now to the imaginative prose with realistic touches of the *Diario de un poeta recien casado* already mentioned, and about which one could write extensively. Jiménez has been writing these brief, poetical prose passages since the beginning of his literary career. They appear in some of his anthologies, in single leaf publications where a considerable part of his work was published, both verse and prose, like the series of broadsides that appeared in 1929. Two aspects of his art meet in these: the imaginative, the lyrical expression almost to the point of delirium of the unreal and an acute observation of reality, of people and their actions. (Read for example, *Ciegos de Madrid*.) All through this one finds, and in the most natural manner, the play of forms, things and colors—for one should not forget that Juan Ramón Jiménez began to look at reality as a painter and there is nothing that will sharpen the faculty of observation more, nothing that will teach us to "see" more than painting. For this reason he has been able to see the countryside and its objects, with his eyes through which penetrate color, lines, form and volume of trees and flowers. And this optical sensibility is united in the poet with an interior hypersensitivity, being as it were the antennae of his spirit, absorbing all that is about it after accurately registering it.

His literary criticism should not be overlooked when one examines the entire work of Juan Ramón Jiménez. In his early years he began writing it in *Helios,* the magazine in which he put such enthusiasm and in whose pages—in the issue of July, 1903—an article appeared on the *Soledades,* the first book of poetry by Antonio Machado. A study of modernism, and to a certain extent of all Spanish poetry, cannot be achieved without reading the critical articles of Juan Ramón, for they are particularly revealing of his times, as for example his lecture on Valle-Inclán, or his pages dedicated to Martí, Darío and Silva. These names lead us to another important book, *Españoles de tres mundos,* Buenos Aires, 1942. It is a volume made up of "lyrical caricatures" as they are called by Jiménez, of writers and artists of the "old world, the new world and the world beyond," that is to say those living in Spain and America and those from here and there who have died, described in brief pages in his most alive, nervous prose with traces at times resembling Valle-Inclan's rugged "esperpentos," while other traces suggest the poetic mood, or sometimes with a raising of the subject to high praise or descending to the ridiculous in word pictures that are biting, bitter, a Goyesque etching. All manner of things can be found in this book, since it is a summation and recounting of many persons and things and places he admired and some he despised, so that the reading of it is necessary if we wish to become acquainted with a countless number of people seen through the impassioned eyes of the author.

Of greater critical breadth and depth are his lectures on *Poesía y literatura, Aristocracia y democracia, Una política poética, La razón heroica, Quemarnos del todo,* some of which can be read in their first English translation in this book, and which represent the fundamental thought of Juan Ramón Jiménez, together with his love for the humble aspects of life, the attention he pays to the simple ways of men, the joy of creating poetry by watering a plant or listening to the sound of water, or that example of a taxi-driver who treated his motor as a human being. As I have already observed, Juan Ramón Jiménez is a poet of "essence" (extra-poet) over and above the limits bound by poetry. And he reaches beyond poetry sometimes to touch philosophical thought. His essay *La razón heroica* is an example. Here we find thoughts on the place of the poet in society, the poet as a creative being, as the sum of general human experience, as a man within his social sphere, as an expression of that society in any given instant of its evolution. We see that Juan Ramón is not a writer living outside of his historical period, as some believe him to be. His critical attitude, the personal one in moments of "politi-

cal" decisions in his life, reveal the profound historicity of this
writer fixed to an epoch, a country and a democratic credo with-
out concessions or vacillations.

Criticism of events and people has not prevented Jiménez
from criticizing himself in the most severe manner; the constant
dissatisfaction in his work can explain and justify his dissatisfac-
tion with the work of others. He punished others at times with an
irritable pen; but his self-criticism is no less violent. Whoever
wishes to examine this criticism has only to read some of the in-
numerable aphorisms strewn throughout many pages of his writ-
ings, collected in some parts of his anthologies or published in
single sheets. There, as grains of sand, each one separate and
brilliant, are all the imaginable forms of criticism and the most
varied facets of a non-conformist spirit, always in constant evolu-
tion and change, yet the same. There also can be found the young
poet's melancholy and the ailing sensitivity of one who left Mo-
guer of Andalusia one day in 1900 and has since filled the Spanish
speaking world with poetry.

4

Another aspect of Juan Ramón Jiménez's work that holds un-
doubted importance in our contemporary, literary history is the
role he has played as mentor for the young. All the present day
critics agree on this; not only those of our language but foreign
critics who have followed his work. They all affirm that Juan
Ramón Jiménez has been the most powerful and effective tie
in uniting Rubén Darío with our present day poets (E. Allison
Peers), since he was capable of absorbing from modernism
those enduring elements or those of greatest value for the future
of Spanish poetry and he passed these on to a younger genera-
tion who gathered about him, not to receive orders, for he gave
none (José Moreno Villa) but to receive inspiration and above
all to look closely at the living example of an almost heroic de-
votion to poetry. This has been his great influence, to encourage

a serious, demanding work of universal value. We also know, because Federico de Onís mentioned it years ago, that if poetry in the Spanish language enters into modernism through Rubén Darío, it is by Juan Ramón Jiménez that it departs from it, so much so that both poets are the two poles around which all our contemporary poetry revolves. On the other hand, that English authority on Hispanism, J. B. Trend, tells us that Juan Ramón Jiménez has done many things his contemporaries did, only that he has done them first, such as the modern use of the metaphor, the play of words, the magical combination of sounds.

Jiménez himself has recognized with complete objectivity as he observes the panorama of this half century of poetry in the Spanish speaking countries that the four most influential names have been Rubén Darío, Juan Ramón Jiménez, Pablo Neruda and Federico García Lorca, each more so perhaps in a given moment or in a section of poetry, or as seems natural, in similar temperaments. In many cases it has been and still is plain imitation; in others—and this is the important fact—it is the influence, purified and assimilated by those poets of true personality and of an original voice. But there has always existed a moment, in almost all of them, in which the modernistic accent, first, or the one of Jiménez, Neruda or Lorca, either successively or independently have been apparent.

One must keep in mind, moreover, that all the great Spanish poets of today, that brilliant generation that began to publish in the decade of 1920-1930, have been breathing more or less the poetic air of Juan Ramón Jiménez; and that the best known of them, Lorca, began his career in a tone and style close to that of *Arias tristes* by Jiménez, while Salinas and Guillén show, on occasion, some echoes of the master's accent.

It is clear that the influence of Juan Ramón Jiménez, along with that of Rubén Darío, has been the most profound when it is not limited, as with Salinas and Guillén, to a given *manner*, but is nearer to that which in Jiménez is a way of understanding poetry, a philosophy of the poetic, a fundamental attitude before the lyrical, the absolute self-deliverance to his world and the daily expression of this world through the medium of poetry. Toward this end, Jiménez from his early years in Madrid began to publish his own works along with the work of others, editing several magazines, the first of which *Helios,* already mentioned, is one of the most important contributions to the triumph of modernism in Spain. Later on, he published others, such as *Indice, Si,* always counting on the collaboration of poets younger than himself whom he has known how to stimulate and reassure in their literary careers. The task of bringing together younger writers through their work—even though some of them later separated from each other or violently clashed with him—the task of orienting them and getting them on their way, Jiménez did in Cuba in 1936-1937, bringing out the poems of those of us who were younger in an anthology along with older writers and with some seldom published at that time. Whether they later continued or not is of no great importance. The task of grouping was accomplished and from the poet's short stay in Havana an example exists, an anthology of Cuban poetry, for which we may be grateful since in it all of us could see our affinities and differences pointed out to us before we could grasp them in the prologue he wrote for the book. It is significant that this prologue demonstrates the acuteness of vision and certitude in judgment of the Spanish poet in understanding the position poetry occupied in Cuba at that given moment in its history. He would also have accomplished the same work in Buenos Aires in 1948 where he was invited to give some lectures, had he resided there for some time; and he has accomplished it in Puerto Rico in these last years in spite of his illnesses and periods of retirement. Because of this, Cintio Vitier, the Cuban poet and critic, has recently said—and his words reach out beyond the immediate surroundings of his country to embrace all the panorama of Spanish contemporary poetry—that Juan Ramón Jiménez

"is our consummate poetical father, who thrust open for us the real doors of life, and showed us the countryside and creatures emerging from the fogs of their original dawn, who gave a name to things and placed them in our ardent, tremulous, hands, the very things, rainbow-hued, sad, or happy at being what they were,"

because "if Darío made again a golden language, Juan Ramón Jiménez has made it again one of light."

Eugenio Florit

Any attempt to present the work of a foreign poet in English raises the objection that poetry can not be translated. In the larger sense this is of course true. One can never capture the precise resonance which a subtle interplay of sound and meaning creates in the poet's own language. The poet here translated, Juan Ramón Jiménez, is a fine musician and he writes in a language which has great poetic assets. Spanish is richer in feminine endings than is English; likewise words ripple with many syllables whose counterparts in the latter tongue are monosyllabic and abrupt. Much of the authentic music therefore cannot be brought over. Granting all this, certain things still can be attempted and for good reasons.

Jiménez is a poet who has dedicated his whole life to his art.

He emerges a consistent figure, an unwavering force, a robust statement of value. He is a kind of spiritual Atlas bearing the burden of culture in a society in which culture is beset by many dehumanizing forces. His heroic task has long been appreciated by his own Spanish-speaking world, but now, with international honors coming to him late in life, he is still virtually unknown to the American public. It is important therefore to present not a few poems but a fairly large body of work. Faithful rendering can recreate in English the freer forms in which many of the poems are written and suggest the more strict ones (no attempt has been made to rhyme the sonnets and other formal lyrics). Then, too, the characteristic imagery can be reproduced which creates Jiménez's style, a style which becomes more and more refined as certain words and concepts appear and reappear, acquiring a continually deeper symbolic significance. Once in a while, too, when the muses are in a particularly good mood, a poem in English results which is not unworthy of the original.

A truly representative group of poems and prose pieces has therefore been assembled here and translated on these terms. Indeed a foreign poet's work has seldom been so extensively presented. The collection should be viewed as a whole. If it is approached from this point of view it will be seen that this selection from half a century of writing paints a portrait, a portrait extending through time, a portrait of the spiritual life of Juan Ramón Jiménez.

Jiménez has in many cases reworked and republished various poems in subsequent "anthologies." As a result, the date of composition is sometimes uncertain. In this collection the individual poems are assigned the date of the book in which they first appeared. The work entitled "Unidad" consists of eight groups of twelve unbound sheets, each in a numbered binder with the poet's signature and the date, 1925.

H. R. Hays

1

1900-1915/Early, Traditional and Modernistic Poems

NOCTURNE

. . . The garden is deserted.
The avenues lead off to
The uncertain penumbra
Of far away foliage.
The twilight has consumed
Its holocaust of scarlet
And from fountains of sky—
Founts of blossoming waters—
Breezes from the countries
Of slumber bear down to earth
A fragrance of new lilies,
A coolth of tenuous airs . . .

The trees are not moving;
Their calm is so human
They seem more alive
Than when their branches are waving.
. . . And in transparent waves
Of the green zenith wander
Mysticisms of a sigh
And a perfume of prayers—

How sad to love everything
And not to know what we love!
. . . It seems that the stars
Speak to me with pity
But are so far away
I cannot understand their words—
How sad to possess the sacred
Soul's garden, blossomless,
To dream of souls in flower,
To dream of gentle smiles,
Of sweet eyes, of evenings
In fantastic spring seasons!
How sad to weep without eyes
That answer our tears,
Feeling all through the night
As if eyes were staring at them!
. . . Night has entered, the air
Bears a perfume of acacias
And of roses; the garden puts its flowers
To sleep . . . tomorrow,
When the moon hides away
And serenity of dawn
Gives the world the soft kiss
Of its lilies and breezes,
These solitary paths

Will be flooded with joy;
Lovers coming for roses
To give to their sweethearts
And children and birds
Shall play gaily . . . wings
Of gold see no life
Through a cloud of tears!

. . . Who could dissolve himself
In this indeterminate hue
Which floods space with its waves,
Pure, pale, and fragrant!
Ah if this world were but always
A perfumed evening,
I would lift it to the skies
In the chalice of my soul!

Rimes/1900-1902

AUTUMN ARIA

River of crystal, sleeping
And enchanted: sweet valley,
Sweet shores of white elm trees
And of green willows.

There is a dream and a heart
In the valley: it dreams and it knows
How to grant with its dreams a languid
Sound of flutes and ballads.

6

Enchanted river, the sleepy
Branches of the willows,
Trailing in the eddies,
Kiss the clear crystals.

And the sky is placid and soft,
A low floating sky
Which with mists of silver
Caresses trees and waters.

My heart has been dreaming
With the shores and the valley
And has come to the quiet bank
To set sail at last;

But descending the footpath
It wept with love in an old air
An unknown someone was singing
In another valley.

Arias tristes/ 1902-1903

NOCTURNE

The moon pours a stream of glitter
Into the depths of my soul
Leaving me the same as
A sweet and tempered pool.

7

Then my depths, good
For everyone, rising, rising,
Spread their water of lights
At the brim of the world's meadow.

Water, uniting star and flower,
Incites to thirst with celestial
Splendors in which are blue kingdoms
Shipwrecked by love.

Arias tristes/1902-1903

GALANTE GARDEN: I

Spring morning!
She came to kiss me
Just as a morning skylark
Soared up from the furrow singing,
"Spring morning!"

I spoke to her of a white butterfly
That I saw in the footpath;
And she gave me a rose
And said, "How I love you!
Don't you know that I love you?"

So many kisses she cherished
On her red lips for me!

I was kissing her eyelids . . .
"My eyes are for you
And you for my red lips!"

The spring heavens
Were blue with peace and oblivion . . .
A morning skylark
Sang in the still sleeping garden . . .
Its voice was light and crystal
In the newplowed furrow . . .
Spring morning!

Jardines lejanos/1903-1904

GALANTE GARDEN: II

There was no one. The water—no one?
How can the water be no one? There is
No one. There's the flower—is no one there?
But is the flower no one?

There is no one. There was the wind—no one?
Is the wind no one? There is
No one. Illusion—is no one there?
And is the illusion no one?

Jardines lejanos/1903-1904

SORROWFUL GARDEN

You will look at me weeping—
It will be in the time of flowers—
You will look at me weeping,
And I shall say to you: don't weep.

My heart, slowly,
Will fall fast asleep . . . your hand
Will tenderly caress
Your brother's perspiring forehead.

You will look at me and suffer,
I alone shall have your pain;
You will look at me and suffer,
You, sister, who are so good to me.

And you will say to me: what is it?
And I shall look at the ground.
And you will say to me: what is it?
And I shall look up at the sky.

And I shall smile—
And you will be frightened—
And I shall smile
As if saying: it's nothing at all . . .

Jardines lejanos / 1903-1904

PASTORALE

Here come the wagons now . . .
The wind and the pinegrove have said so,
The golden moon has said so,
The smoke and the echo have said so . . .
These are the wagons passing
After sunset, on these evenings,
The wagons that are bearing
Dead tree-trunks down from the mountain.

How the wagons are weeping
Along the Pueblo Nuevo Road!

By the light of the bright stars
The oxen come dreaming
Of the warm stable
With its savor of maternity and hay.
And behind the wagons
The drovers come walking
With their goads over their shoulders
And their eyes fixed on the sky.

How the wagons are weeping
Along the Pueblo Nuevo Road!

Through the peace of the country
The dead tree-trunks, as they pass,
Leave a fresh and honest odor
Of heartwood laid open.
And the sound of the Angelus falls
From the tower of the old hamlet
Over the meadows,
With a graveyard odor.

How the wagons are weeping
Along the Pueblo Nuevo Road!

Pastorales/1903-1905

PASTORALE

Pomegranates in the blue sky,
Street of the mariners,
How green are your trees,
How joyful you make the sky!

Illusory wind from the sea,
Street of the mariners—
Grey eye, lock of gold,
Dark and ruddy features!

The woman sings in the doorway,
"The life of the mariners,
A man always at sea
And the heart in the wind."

Virgin of Carmel, may the oars
Always rest in your hands;
Under your eyes may the sea
Be calm and the sky blue!

In the evening the air gleams:
The west is made of dreams;

It is a gold of nostalgia
Of revery and tears.

As if the wind were bearing
Endlessness and in its restless
Yearning they were looking
And listening for those far away.

Illusory wind from the sea,
Street of the mariners,
The blue blouse and the saint's medal
Ribbon around the chest!

Pomegranates in the blue sky,
Street of the mariners,
A man always at sea,
And the heart in the wind!

Pastorales/1903-1905

The afternoon roads
Become one at night.
By it I must go to you,
Love, so securely hidden.

By it I must go to you,
Like the light on the mountains,

Like the breeze from the sea,
Like the fragrance of flowers.

El valle/1903-1905

(THE POET HAS DIED IN THE COUNTRY)

The sun will gild the leaves,
Sprinkle diamonds on the river,
Make a song of gold and laughter
With the wind in the pine trees.

With their lips filled with roses,
Children will run into the garden,
Its golden dream broken,
Its dream of maidens and lilies.

He who bears the sad news
Through the dust of the highway
Will see white butterflies
And crystals of dewdrops:

"Maria . . . God with you . . . Good day!"
You happy and blossoming village,
You will go on filling with sunshine,
With white smoke, with blue smoke,
With bells and with idyls.

All will move toward midday
In peace and love . . . in the pine trees

A bird will be singing . . . and everything
Will be yellow and silent.

El valle/1903-1905

Among the clouds the moon is
A shepherdess of silver
Who, through pathways of stars,
Drives her white gleaming flocks.

The sky offers her blue lagoons
And smooth-worn cattlepaths
Full of snowy rosebushes
And secluded cottages.

Ah sweet cattle-waterers
Of the horizon, clear streams,
Backwaters of eternity,
Green wandering shores!

In friendship, she comes close, for a moment
To all things: doorways, sheepfolds,
Rivulets, roses, shores . . .
And goes on, goes on nostalgically.

Flowering swamps
Where thunders the soft bellow

Of white constellations,
A herd of white cattle!

The moon goes by slowly,
Naked, lovely, in ecstasy,
Singing to an unknown earth
Along her highways of dawn.

La estrella del pastor/1903-1905

PASTORALE

For heaven's sake be silent,
You shall never know how to say it!
Let all my dreams open
And all my lilies!

My heart can easily hear
The letter of your tenderness . . .
The water flows rippling with it
Between the flowers of the river;
The mist moves dreaming with it,
The pine trees are singing it—
And the rosy moon—and the
Heart of your mill . . .

For heaven's sake don't quench
The flame burning within me!

Be silent, for heaven's sake,
You shall never know how to say it!

Pastorales / 1903-1904

ROOM

How quiet objects are
And how well we manage with them!
Everywhere their hands
Reach out and touch our hands.

How many discreet caresses;
What respect for ideas;
And with what ecstasy they behold
The dream we are dreaming!

How much they like what we like,
How willingly they await
Our return, and how sweetly
They smile at us, half-unfolded!

Objects—friends, sisters;
Women—truth contented,
Jealous, you give us in return
The most fleeting stars!

Olvidanzas / 1906-1907

MORNING OF THE CROSS

NOTE: *The cross of spring is a folk custom which takes place on the third of May. A cross of flowers is set up in the streets, on the house-fronts, or in the patios in Spanish towns. It coincides with the fiesta of the Holy Cross and announces the entrance of spring.* ED.

God is blue. The flute and the drum
Are announcing the cross of spring.
Long live the roses, the roses of love,
In the green and gold of the meadows!

Let us go to the fields for rosemary,
Let us go, let us go
For rosemary and love . . .

I asked her, "May I love you?"
She answered, radiant with passion,
"When the cross of spring blossoms,
I shall love you with all my heart."

Let us go to the fields for rosemary,
Let us go, let us go
For rosemary and love . . .

"Now the cross of spring has blossomed.
Love, the cross, the cross, love, has blossomed!"
She answered, "you wish me to love you?"
And the morning light transfixed me!

Let us go to the fields for rosemary,
Let us go, let us go
For rosemary and love . . .

The flute and drum gladden our banner.
The butterfly brings us illusion . . .

My love is the corn maiden,
She will love me with all her heart!

Baladas de primavera/1907

THE DISTANT SEA

The fountain's cantata is fading.
All the roadways awaken . . .
Silver sea, sea of daybreak,
How pure you look through the pine trees!

Southern wind, are you coming
Sonorous with suns? The roadways are blinded . . .
Sea of siesta-time, golden sea,
How gay you are over the pine trees!

The green finch is saying an unknown something . . .
My soul goes off on the roadways . . .
Afternoon sea, rosy sea,
How calm you look through the pine trees!

Baladas de primavera/1907

WALKING

Dream

Walking, walking;
How I love to hear each grain
Of sand I am treading.

Walking, walking;
Leave the horses behind,
I would rather come late, lingering—
Walking, walking—
Giving my soul to each grain
Of earth I am treading.

Walking, walking.
How sweet to enter my own fields,
Huge night just descending.

Walking, walking,
Now my heart is a backwater;
I am what is awaiting me—
Walking, walking—
And it seems my foot is caressing
My heart warmly.

Walking, walking;
How I long to see all the tears
Of this road I am singing!

Baladas de primavera/1907

GREEN GREENFINCH

Green greenfinch
Sweetens the setting sun!

Palace of enchantment,
The pine grove at evening
Hushes with tears
The flight of the river.
Yonder the greenfinch
Has its shady nest.

Green greenfinch
Sweetens the setting sun!

The last breeze
Is just a breath;
The red sun sheds iridescence
On the weeping pine.
Dim and slow
Is the hour, greenfinch!

Green greenfinch
Sweetens the setting sun!

Solitude and calm,
Silence and greatness.
The cabin of the soul
Collects itself and prays.
Suddenly, oh beauty,
The greenfinch sings!

Green greenfinch
Sweetens the setting sun!

Its song enraptures.
Has the wind ceased?
The country fills
With its emotion.
Mallow-pink is the lament,
Green the greenfinch

Green greenfinch
Sweetens the setting sun!

Baladas de primavera/1907

ELEGY OF PURITY

I love the green landscape by the shore of the river.
Between the green boughs sun fills the west with illusion;
And over the golden flowers my own reveries,
A twilight of the soul, are flowing with the current.

To the sea? To the sky? To the world? Who knows? The stars
Descend, as usual to the river, carried by the breezes . . .
The nightingale meditates . . . Sorrow grows more lovely,
And high above sadness a smile bursts into bloom.

Elejías/1907-1908

ELEGIAC LAMENT: I

Infancy, green meadow, belltower, palmtree,
Many-colored oriel, sun, wandering butterfly
Who used to hover in the spring-scented evening
At the blue zenith, a rosy-hued caress!

Enclosed garden in which a bird was singing
Among the foliage tinged with melodious golds,
Cool and soothing breeze upon which there came to me
The faint and distant music of the bullring!

. . . Before that nameless bitterness of failure
Came to garland my suffering heart with mourning,
As a child I loved the nightingale in the clear evening,
Everyone's silence or the voice of the fountain.

Elejías/1907-1908

ELEGIAC LAMENT: II

Oh sad old carriage rolling through my memories!
Village that disappears into a corner of my soul!
Great and pure tear, dawnstar that lingers
Trembling on the hilltop above the green fields!

Green and profound sky; the road used to waken,
Fragrant and cool in the charm of the hour,

Rousing, a nightingale used to warble, and the watermill
Meditated an eternal sound, pink-browed against sunrise.

And in the soul a memory, a tear and a hand
Raising a white curtain as the carriage passed . . .
Road of last evening blue beneath the solitary
Moon, and the kisses of the last night of all . . .

Oh sad old carriage rolling through my memory!
Village that disappears into a corner of my soul!
Great and pure tear, dawnstar that lingers
Trembling on the hilltop above the green fields!

Elejías/1907-1908

DEEP AND SLEEPING WATER

Deep and sleeping water, you who seek no glory,
Who have disdained to be fiesta or cataract;
Who, when the eyes of the moon caress you,
Fill yourself wholly with silver reflections . . .

Water, silent and pure with sorrowful eddies,
Who have despised the glitter and the sonorous triumph,
Who, when the warm sweet sun penetrates you,
Fill yourself wholly with golden reflections . . .

Lovely and profound you are, you are like my soul;
To your peace sorrows have come to meditate

24

And there are born on the placid shores of your serenity
The purest examples of wings and of flowers.

La soledad sonora/1908

Ah how softly the brook
Trickles, the water drips
From flower to flower
Like a butterfly that sings.

An instant it seduces
Each flower, kisses it, strings it
On a chain and each whispers
Some moist deception.

It holds a mirror to their silks—
They lend it fragrance—
It seems it will never
Wish to depart; they play and they chatter
And the madrigal of coolness
Goes wrapped in the grace
Of a sweet golden rose
Of setting sun . . .
                What a bright
Iridescence of harmonies!
Ah, what purity!
                And the water goes

From flower to flower
Like a butterfly that sings.

La flauta en el arroyo/1908

NUDES

(Adieus. Absence. Return.)

The moon was born grey, and Beethoven was weeping
Beneath her white hands, within her piano . . .
In the unlit living room, she was, as she played,
Dark with moonlight and three times as lovely.

The flowers of our two hearts were bleeding to death
And perhaps we wept without either seeing the tears . . .
Each note set afire one of the wounds of love . . .
The sweet piano endeavored to understand us.

From the balcony, open to the misty starlight,
A sad wind came, from invisible worlds . . .
And she, she asked me about things unknowable
And I answered her with unattainable things.

La soledad sonora/1908

YELLOW SPRING

April came, full
Of yellow flowers.
The brook was yellow,
The stone walls were yellow, the hill,
The children's graveyard,
And the orchard where love was living.

The sun anointed the world with yellow,
With downpouring rays,
Ah, through the golden lilies,
The warm golden water,
The yellow butterflies
Over the golden roses.

Yellow garlands were climbing
Up the trees, the day
Was a grace perfumed with gold
In a golden awakening of life.
Among the bones of the dead,
God opened his yellow hands.

Poemas májicos y dolientes/1909

FRANCINA IN THE GARDEN
(. . . *Rit de la fraîcheur de l'eau.—V. Hugo*)

With lilacs full of water
I struck her shoulders.

And all of her white flesh
Was jewelled with clear droplets.

Ah moist and snowy flight
Over the pearly sand!

Her flesh died away palely
Among the scarlet rosebushes,

Like a silver apple,
Frost-covered at dawn.

She ran flying from the water
Among the scarlet rosebushes.

And she laughed, fantastically.
Her laughter, too, was moistened . . .

With lilacs full of water,
As she ran, I beat her.

Poemas májicos y dolientes/1909

DREAM SEASCAPE

The stormy sky, heavy and full of echoes,
Splits open in the west. A sharp knife of light,
Acrid and ambiguous, adorns the fearful instant
With a strange splendor, delirious and yellow.

What the light wounds, like a cry bursts into flame;
The high, rocky coast is carmine and golden;
The galleys are set on fire and a livid flame
Runs over the black waves, tragically mad.

Furious, the wind strikes, profound and tormented,
Against the iridescence of the distorted day;
And in a fantastic allegory, in the depths of the east
A false and gilded sun sheds its insistent rays . . .

Poemas májicos y dolientes/1909

PERFUME AND NOSTALGIA

It used to be in summer. The old carriage
Carried the others away . . . And the tranquil evening
Went on fading among the meadows of the night
With a murmur of pine trees and a complaint of cattlebells.

The carriage appeared with a barking of greyhounds
At the fragrant bend of the sandy roadway.
The "good-bys" were lost among the jingling bells . . .
We were left behind alone in the quiet hour.

Silence you surged from us. Hands
Whiter than the moonlight slackened their desire
And, among the pine groves, our eyes, close by,
Grew gradually larger than the sea and the sky.

Poemas májicos y dolientes/1909

FIFTH CHORD

With nothing remembered . . .
Let the still night fall asleep
Like a great flock,
Soft and black-veiled . . .

Let no word be spoken . . .
Let the loved woman fly
Through the thick-carpeted
Dream-haunted dwelling . . .

With nothing longed for . . .
Be lost in the holy idea
Just as a gilded
Cloud fades at sunrise.

Arte menor/1909

NUDES

From the sea there will come
The flowers of dawn—
Waves, waves full of
Snowy lilies—
The cock shall be sounding
His silver clarion.

Today! I shall tell you,
Touching your soul.

Oh under the pine trees
Your mallow-pink nakedness,
Your feet in the tender
Frost-rimed grass,
Your hair all green with
Moistened stars!

And you will tell me,
Flying: tomorrow!

The cock shall be sounding
His clarion, full of
Flames and daybreak,
Singing in scarlets,
He will set his fires
In the smooth branches . . .

Today! I shall tell you,
Touching your soul.

Oh in the newborn sun
Your gilded tears,
The enormous eyes
In your elfin face,
Ardent, avoiding
My sable glances!

And you will tell me,
Flying: tomorrow!

Arte menor / 1909

IDYL

The green, flowering earth
Of the new cemetery
Received you this morning,
In its cool heart.

When I left I saw
A rainbow like your hair,
By which you were climbing
To a canticle of fire,
Ascending to the clear sky,
Widely opened.

Languid springtime!
Tender love, cut off!
You saw none of this
You laughingly said!

You took but one journey:
From the village to the heavens.

Los rincones plácidos/1909

THE WHEAT-EAR

The wheat is golden-grained in the clear daylight,
Setting afire its close-packed treasure in radiance;
But it grows sorrowful and in miserly arrogance
Discontentedly spills its riches over the earth.

The rich grain reopens in the friendly shadow
Of the moistened earth—cradle and tomb, fecund exchange—
To spring up again in other, finer wheat-ears,
Still fuller, still firmer, still taller, more golden.

And . . . back to the earth again, desire unquenchable,
Attuned to one measure alone, the perfect wheat-ear,
The one supreme form which raises the soul to
The unattainable, oh poetry, infinite, aureate, upright!

Poemas agrestes: 2/1910-1911

THE CONCLUSIVE VOYAGE

I shall go away. And the birds will still be there,
Singing,
And my garden will be there with its green tree
And its white well.

Each afternoon the sky will be blue and peaceful,
And the notes will ring out as this afternoon they ring out
From the bells of the belltower.

And those who love me will be dead,
And the village will renew itself each year,
And in the corner of my flowering, whitewashed garden,
My spirit shall wander nostalgically . . .

And I shall go away; and be alone, homeless, with no
Green tree, with no white well,

33

With no blue and peaceful sky,
And the birds will still be there, singing.

Corazón en el viento/1910-1911

NEW LEAVES

To Isoldita Esplá

Look how the golden children
Are climbing the silver poplars to the sky!
And they go, staring at the sky,
As they climb in the blue their eyes like pure dreams,
Look how the golden children
Are climbing up the silver poplars to the sky!
And the blue of their lovely
Eyes and the sky are touching . . . eyes and sky are one!
Look how the golden children
Are climbing the silver poplars to the sky!

Corazón en el viento/1910-1911

PORTRAIT OF AN UNSEASONABLE TIME

How eternal the grass is at night when the cricket
Sings under the celestial silence of the moon!

The world goes spinning into daybreak
Through a western sky white with wandering clouds.

Cities of crystal, of white lilies, of marble,
Recede in a dream of summits of coolness;
And the hills are bordered with motionless silver
And some unknown nostalgia of disturbed graveyards.

All is falling, weeping senselessly, the moments
Die away, splendidly in flight . . .
Stately, at the edge of the meadow, a pale sad face
Meditates, dazzled by a dying moon.

Laberinto/1910-1911

ODOR OF JASMINE

What a sadness, as in the odor of jasmine!
Summer returns to burn the streets, darken the houses,
And at night trickling rays of starlight
Heavily weigh on eyelids laden with nostalgia.

On the balconies, white, silent women linger
Until late at night, resembling fantasms;
Sometimes the river sends forth a tired breeze,
Perhaps is a romantic and unattainable music.

The penumbra glistens with sighs, the world
Becomes, in a magical forgetfulness, afloat in the soul;

And dragonflies are caught in languid hands,
And the high moon stagnates among the constellations.

What a sadness there is in the odor of jasmine!
Pianos are opened, there are warm glances
Everywhere . . . In the depths of each azure shadow
A passionate and languid vision dissolves.

Laberinto/1910-1911

TENEBRAE

All of the west is lemon yellow.
At the closed zenith, under the mute clouds,
Black flocks of melancholy birds constantly
Trace lines over the false sky of rainclouds.

In the somber garden, the roses acquire
A purple velvet from the leaden nimbus,
And the wandering twilight which alters verities
Covers everything it touches, spreading unknown moist vapors.

Livid, dazzled with the yellow, gloomy from the leaden
Light, in my ears a monotonous refrain
Buzzes like a fly, nor do I know where it comes from . . .
Leaving behind it tears . . . which say, "Never . . . never . . ."

Melancolía/1910-1911

DROWNED

August

Her nakedness and the sea!
How they are fulfilled, one
The peer of the other!
                    The water was waiting
Over the centuries
To set her body alone
Upon its huge throne.
And it happened here in Iberia.
The smooth Celtic beach
As if in play gave her
To the summer rollers.
So the smile grows,
Love, to delight.
Behold, mariners,
Venus is queen once more!

Versos, a, por, para/1911

THE DEAD GIRL

Your little cold head
Is like a cut magnolia.
Like an April lily
You have grown in death, in a tragic
Snowy springtime.
All is cut short for you,

And in the white, shining
Coffin, false lap of mock orange,
You lie as if painted—
Charcoal sketch by some sad painter—
Alas, only black and white!
Speak, why do you vanish,
With your lovely future, when already you took part
In the illusion of the world?
Ruined shape, ruined hope!
Only a wandering vapor
Of decay stifled
By strong perfumes . . .
Only a snowwhite silence,
A few lengthening hours
That will come to be
Like the others, tomorrow . . .
And you, cold, supine,
Extinguished, erased!
Fallen moon, tell me,
If it is not a soul, what do you lack.

Poemas impersonales/1909-1912

SKY BEHIND THE BLUE SKY

What fear in the blue of the sky!
Blackness!
Blackness of day, in August!
What fear!

What terror in the blue siesta!
Blackness.
Blackness in the roses and the river!
What fear!

Blackness of day, in my country—
Blackness!
Above the white walls!
What fear!

Emoción/1912-1913

Sunday afternoons in winter
When everyone has gone out!
The pure, yellow-green sun
Penetrates to the cold corners
And into the roses,
Just tended this morning—the light
Is listening,
Spotless with love.
                    The perfect hour
Resembles one of my books.
And I go smiling through the whole house alone,
Savoring my soul,
Picking up and kissing the fallen crumbs.

Bonanza/1911-1912

WINTER SONG

Singing. Singing.
Where are the birds that are singing?

It has rained. And still the branches
Have no new leaves. Singing. Birds
Are singing. Where are the birds
That are singing?

I have no birds in cages.
There are no children who sell them. Singing.
The valley is far away. Nothing . . .

I do not know where the birds are
That are singing—singing, singing—
The birds that are singing.

Canciones/1910-1911

ASH OF ROSES

To all of my calling your name
You have answered with a slow echo . . .
But where are you, woman who now are mine;
Where are you for I can not see you?

Garden of ineffable memories,
West of dreams, of dreams to come,

Breeze which carries things nearest
When they live farthest away,
Shall I walk through life now
Groping, like a blind man?

Yes, to all my sighs
You have answered with a gentle sighing . . .
You are here, you are here,
You intoxicate me, I sense you!
But where are you, woman who now are mine,
Where are you for I can not see you?

La frente pensativa/1911-1912

Who knows what is on the opposite side of each hour!
How many times has the dawn been
Behind a mountain!
How many times has the royal conflagration of a horizon
Held thunder in its golden heart!
That rose was poison.
That sword gave life.
I thought a blossoming
Meadow was at the end of a road
And I discovered a morass.
I dreamed of the glory of the human
And I found myself in the divine.

La frente pensativa/1911-1912

LOVE

You are not dead, no.
        You are reborn
With the roses, in every spring.
Like life, you have
Your dry leaves;
You have your snow, like
Life . . .
    But your earth,
Love, is sown with
Profound promises
Which must be fulfilled even in the same
Forgetfulness.
       The attempt not to love is vain.
The sweet breeze one day returns to the soul;
A night of stars,
And you descend, love, to the senses,
Chaste as the first time.
Since you are pure, you are
Eternal! Into your presence,
Through the blue, in a white flock,
Gentle doves return that we thought dead . . .
You open each flower with new leaves . . .
You gild the immortal light with new tongues . . .
You are eternal, love,
Like spring!

La frente pensativa/1911-1912

LIGHTNESS

Cities

The curtain,
In the August quietude and the silence
Of the tranquil morning,
Moves gently in the wandering air . . .
Beautiful moment,
A brotherhood between the living and the dead
That confuses them—one doesn't know
Who is living and who dead—
In the same intensity of breath!
All the world is dead, or all
Alive,
And the wandering morning air
Moves the white curtain
Of my open window . . .
It seems,
This movement of the curtain,
Universal life, the breath of all
The earth, the force
Which alone remains
From the flight of the star, its sound
In its celestial orbit.
And the curtain
Moves,
In the wandering morning air,
White . . .
A plenitude of the minimum
Which fills the world and fixes
The immensity of thought
In its vagueness—leaf
Which falls, drop
Which shines,

Praise which passes . . .
And the curtain,
Its whiteness now blue—
For the night is over
In which I watched its moving vagueness—
Moves, gently still, in the wandering air.

Desvelo/1912

WAKEFULNESS

A small village

The sheep was bleating softly.
The gentle ass was rejoicing,
Calling ardently.
The dog was barking
As if speaking to the stars.

I awoke. I went forth. I saw
Celestial prints on the ground,
Flowering
Like a heaven
Inverted.

A warm soft vapor
Was veiling the foliage;
The moon was setting
In a silk and golden west
That seemed a divine region . . .

44

There was a beating in my breast
As if my heart were wine-quickened . . .

I opened the stable to see if
He was there.
                    He was there!

HUGE HOUR

To Oscar Esplá

The peace is disturbed by only the sound of bells, a bird . . .
It seems as if the two are talking to the west.
The silence is golden. The afternoon is of crystal.
A straying purity sets the cool trees swaying.
Beyond all things a limpid river is dreaming,
And, scattering pearls, is flying toward the infinite . . .
Solitude! Solitude! All is clear and muted . . .
The peace is disturbed by only the sound of bells, a bird . . .
Love lives far away . . . serene and indifferent,
The heart is wholly free; it is neither sad nor joyful.
Colors divert it, breezes, songs, and perfumes . . .
It swims as if in a lake immune to feeling.
The peace is disturbed by only the sound of bells, a bird . . .
And it seems as if my hand could seize the eternal.

El silencio de oro/1911-1912

NOTHING

To your abandon I oppose the lofty
Tower of my divine reflections.
The bleeding heart raised up to them
Shall behold the sea, be empurpled by them.

I shall create daybreak in my shadow,
My lyre I shall keep from the insubstantial wind,
I shall seek my food within my inmost being . . .
But, ah, if this peace should be only nothing?

Nothing, yes, nothing, nothing! O should my heart
Sink down into the water then would the world
Become a cold and hollow castle . . .

For you are you, oh human springtime,
The earth, the air, the water, fire, all things!
And I am nothing but my own reflections.

Sonetos espirituales/1914-1915

DISGUST

Like a sick man whose life is despaired of
And who feebly turns his face against the wall,
Resolved to die with resignation,
I turn my back upon your glacial caution.

Many thanks to you, woman. You have given me
More than I deserved. Impertinent caprice
Of a child who believed in madness!
But now I am weary of being grateful.

Your discreet sun which tears open for a moment
The grey sky of January and gently gilds
My pain neither pleases me nor arouses me.

Leave me! Let it all fall down together,
Your conscience and my love, in this hour
That has just struck, infinite and empty!

Sonetos espirituales/1914-1915

BRIEF RETURN

What was she like, good Lord, what was she like?
Oh deceptive heart, Oh indecisive mind!
Was she like the passage of the breeze
Or merely like the fading of springtime?

As light, as fickle, as ephemeral
As summer thistledown . . . yes, undefined
As a smile that loses itself in laughter . . .
In the air as futile as a banner!

Banner, smile, thistledown, winged
June springtime, and the pure breeze . . .
How mad was your carnival and how sad!

All your mutability turned to nothingness—
Memory, blind, buzzing bee of bitterness—
Not knowing what you were, I know that you have been.

Sonetos espirituales/1914-1915

OCTOBER

I laid myself down on the earth in front of
The infinite countryside of Castile,
Autumn was swathing the fields in the yellow
Sweetness shed by the clear light of its sunset.
Slowly the plow in parallel furrows
Spread apart the dark soil and with simple gestures
The open hand was scattering the seed
In its honestly parted inner recesses.
I thought to snatch out my heart and fling it,
Full of its lofty and profound feelings,
Along the broad furrow of tender farmland
To see if, by shredding it and sowing it,
The coming spring would reveal to the world
The tree of love, so pure and eternal.

Sonetos espirituales/1914-1915

TO MY SOUL

You keep the branch always in readiness
For the appropriate rose, you are always
Alert, with your warm ear at the gateway
Of your body, awaiting the unhoped for arrow.

No wave emerges out of nothingness
But it carries with it a better light
From your spreading shadow. At night you are wakeful
Within your star, unveiled to living.

On all things you set an invisible sin,
Then, glorious revisitation of the summits,
You will wholly revive all that bears your seal.

Your rose will be the ideal pattern of roses,
Your ear, pattern of harmony, and your thoughts
Of radiance, your wakefulness of the stars.

Sonetos espirituales / 1914-1915

Everywhere arrows of gold
Are killing the summer. The air
Carries diluted agonies
As the blood carries poisons.
Everything—the wings, the flowers,

The light—goes on a journey.
How many sad farewells!
The heart sets out on the sea.
Shudderings and tears.
Where are you going? Where are you?
Everything asks this of everything.
Nothing and no one knows . . .

Oro/1915

GOLD

(It is engender'd in the eyes;
With gazing fed: and Fancy dies
In the cradle where it lies.—Shakespeare)

You far away, far from yourself,
I much closer to mine;
You outward, toward the earth,
I inward, toward infinity.

The suns you shall see
Are suns seen before;
I shall see new suns
The spirit alone sets afire.

When our faces encounter each other
Nothing they say will be the same.
Your forgetfulness will be in your eyes
But mine will be in my heart.

Estío/1915

CONVALESCENCE

Only you keep me company, friend sun.
Like a dog of light you lick my white bed
And I lose my hand within your golden fur,
Listless with weariness.

How many things that were
Depart . . . ever more distantly!
                                                   I am silent

And I smile, just like a child,
Letting you lick me, tame sun.

All of a sudden, sun, you leap up
And, with an ardent and crazy clamor,
Bark at the fleeting phantoms,
Those mute shadows that menace me
From the desert of the west.

Estío/1915

2

1907-1916/Selections from the book of prose poems, PLATERO AND I

1 / PLATERO

Platero is little, wooly, and soft, so smooth outside that you would say he was all made of cotton without any bones. Only the jet mirrors of his eyes are as hard as two black glass scarabs.

I set him free and he goes into the meadow and gently caresses the little pink, golden, and cerulean flowers with his muzzle, just touching them . . . I call gently, "Platero?" and he comes to me at a joyful little trot and it seems that he is laughing in some imaginary jingle of bells.

He eats whatever I give him. He likes tangerines, muscatel grapes, oil of amber, and dark figs with their crystalline drop of honey.

He is as gentle and finicky as a child, as a girl, but strong and dry inside as if of stone. When I ride him on Sunday through the farthest alleys of the village, the slow peasants, in clean clothes, stop to look at him:

"Steel in 'im . . ."

There is steel in him. Steel and quicksilver at the same time.

2/SPRING

In my morning doze I am annoyed by little creatures setting up a devilish shrieking. Finally, unable to sleep any longer, I desperately fling myself out of bed. Then, as I look out through the open window on the countryside, I realize that it is the birds which are making such a clamor.

I go into the garden and sing a song of thanksgiving to the god of the blue day. A free concert pours from the beaks of birds, refreshing and endless. The swallow's trill ripples from the pond, the blackbird whistles over a fallen orange, the oriole, all aflame, chatters from bush to bush, the blue titmouse bursts into long minute gusts of laughter in the tip of the eucalyptus, and in the big pine tree the sparrows argue impudently.

What a morning it is! The sun fills the earth with its silver and gold gaiety, butterflies of a hundred colors are playing everywhere, among the flowers, about the house (now inside, now outside), at the spring. The countryside everywhere bursts into explosions, into clicking, boiling with new and vigorous life.

It seems as though we were within a great honeycomb of light which is the interior of an immense, warm, flaming rose.

55

3/ THE FLOWER BY THE ROAD

How pure, Platero, how lovely this flower by the roadside! All
the herds pass alongside it (bulls, goats, colts, men) and though
it is so tender and weak it still stands upright, mallow-pink and
delicate on its stone wall, unstained by any impurity.

You have seen it every day when we take the shortcut at the
beginning of the rise, at its green post. Now it has a little bird
beside it which flies up (why?) as we approach, or it is
filled like a shallow cup with clear water from a summer cloud,
now it allows the bee to rob it or the fickle butterfly to adorn it.

This flower lives but a few days, Platero, even though the mem-
ory of it can be eternal. Its life will be but a day of your spring-
time, but a springtime of my life . . . what wouldn't I give to au-
tumn in exchange for this divine flower, so that for our lives it
might every day be a simple unending example?

4/ THE THORN

As he entered the horse pasture he began to limp. I had to dis-
mount . . .

"What's the matter, fellow?"

Platero had lifted his right forehoof a little, showing the frog,
and was putting no weight on it, scarcely touching the hot sand
of the road with the hoof.

With no doubt more care than old Darbon, his veterinary, I
bent his leg back and looked into the red frog. A large green

thorn from a sturdy orange tree was stuck in it like the round head of a little emerald dagger. While I trembled along with Platero's pain, I drew out the thorn and I took the poor thing to the stream with the yellow lilies so that the running water would lick his little wound with its long, pure tongue.

Afterwards we went on toward the white sea, I ahead, he behind, still limping and gently nudging me in the back.

5/THE THREE KINGS

How excited the children were tonight, Platero! We could not get them to bed. In the end sleep captured them, one in the armchair, one on the floor in the chimney corner, Blanca in a low chair, Pepe in the windowseat with his head on the nails studding the door, lest the kings should come by. And now behind this outward surface of life all their sleep can be felt, alive and magical, beating like a great, full, vigorous heart.

Before supper I went up with all of them. What a clamor on the staircase which on other nights frightened them so!

"I'm not afraid of the skylight, Pepe. What about you?" said Blanca, holding my hand very tightly.

And we put all their shoes on the balcony among the drying fruit. And now, Platero, Montemayor, Tita, Maria Teresa, Lolilla, Perico, you and I are going to get dressed up in blankets, quilts, and old hats. At twelve we must go by the children's windows in a masked procession with lights, beating mortars, blowing on trumpets and on the conch shell which was in the back room. You shall go along with me for I am to be Caspar and I shall wear a white cotton beard and you shall wear the Colombian flag, which I got from the house of my uncle, the consul, like a blanket . . . the children suddenly awakened, with the sleep still lingering in the corners of their amazed eyes will peep through the panes in their nightshirts, trembling and marvelling. Afterwards we shall go on in their dreams through the dawn and until tomorrow, when it is already late and the blue sky illuminates them through the shutters, they will run up, half-dressed, to the balcony to take possession of all their treasure.

Last year we laughed heartily. Platero, my little camel, now you will see what fun we are going to have tonight.

NOTE: *Twelfth Night in Spain, and many Spanish-speaking countries, is equivalent to Christmas in the United States, and the Three Kings to Santa Claus.* ED.

6/SCARLET LANDSCAPE

The summit. And yonder is the west, all purple, wounded by its own crystals which make it bleed all over. Slightly reddened, the green pine grove sharpens and the grass and little flowers, transparently aflame in the splendor of the west, make the serene moment pungent with a moist, luminous and penetrating scent.

And I linger, full of ecstasy, in the twilight. Platero, his dark eyes scarlet from the sunset, goes quietly to a pool of carmine, rose, and violet waters, dips his mouth gently into the mirrors which seem to turn liquid as he touches them and a profuse sea of darkish waters of blood pours down his huge throat.

The spot is familiar but the moment transforms it, turns it into something strange, ruined, and monumental. One would say that we are at any moment going to discover an abandoned palace . . . the evening lingers beyond itself and the hour, tinged with eternity, is infinite, peaceful, inscrutable . . .

"Come on, Platero . . ."

7 / THE LITTLE GIRL

The little girl was Platero's delight. Whenever he saw her coming toward him through the lilacs, in her white dress and rice straw hat, softly calling, "Platero, little Platerooo!" the little ass wanted to break his rope and he jumped like a child and brayed madly.

Blindly confident, she crawled under him again and again, gave him little kicks, put her gleaming white hand into his pink mouth studded with large yellow teeth, or, pulling his ears which he put at her disposal, called him by all the playful variations of his name: "Platero, Plateron, Platerillo, Platerete, Platerucho!"

During those long days in which the child sailed down the river in her white cradle toward death, nobody paid any attention to Platero. She, in her delirium called sadly, "Little Platerooo!" In the house, darkened now and full of sighs, the plaintive distant call of her friend could be heard. Oh melancholy summer!

With what richness God endowed you, afternoon of her funeral! September, pink and gold as it is now, was coming to an end. How the bells echoed from the cemetery, when it was over, in the clear west, pathway to glory! I came by the abandoned and moss-grown adobe walls, entered the house through the yard door, and, avoiding everyone, went to the stable and sat down to think with Platero.

8/CHILL

The moon accompanies us, large, round, and pure. In the slumbering meadows some indistinguishable black goats can be seen among the brambles . . . someone silently hides as we pass . . . Above the stone wall a huge almond tree, snowy with blossoms and moonlight, bending down its top in a white cloud, blankets the roadway, shot with March stars. A penetrating odor of oranges . . . moisture and silence . . . the Ravine of the Witches . . .

"Platero . . . how . . . cold it is!"

Platero is trotting, I don't know whether from my fear or his; he enters the brook, steps on the moon and shatters it. It is as if a swarm of clear, crystal roses, trying to stop him, gets entangled in his trot.

And Platero trots uphill, tucking in his rump as if someone were about to overtake him, now feeling the gentle warmth of the approaching village that never seems to be reached.

9/ANGELUS

Platero, look at the way the roses are falling everywhere, blue roses, pink, white ones, colorless ones. You would think that the sky was dissolving into roses. Look at the way my forehead, my shoulders, my hands are covered with roses . . . what shall I do with so many roses?

Do you know perhaps where this smooth-petaled flowering comes from (I don't know where it comes from) which softens the landscape every day and leaves it faintly pink, white, or cerulean (more roses, more roses) like a picture by Fra Angelico who painted glory on his knees?

One would think that roses were being tossed to earth from the seven tiers of Paradise. Like snow, gentle pale-tinted roses cover the tower, the roof tiles, the trees. Look, everything rough becomes delicate when they decorate it. More roses, more roses, more roses . . .

Platero, as the Angelus sounds, it seems that this quotidian life of ours loses its power and another loftier, purer, more constant force from within makes all things rise, as fountains of grace, to the stars which are set alight among the roses . . . more roses . . . your eyes which you can not see, Platero, which you raise submissively to heaven, are two lovely roses.

10/ THE PARSLEY CROWN

"Let's see who gets there first!"

The prize was a book of prints I had received the day before from Vienna.

"Let's see who gets to the violets first! One . . . two . . . three!"

The children dashed off at a run, a happy tumult of pink and white in the yellow sun. For a moment, in the silence which the mute straining of their chests created in the morning, the slow hour chiming from the village clock could be heard, the minute song of a mosquito on the hill of pine trees which was filled with blue lilies, and the coming and going of the water in the brook . . . the children got to the first orange trees when Platero, who was idling nearby, became infected with the game and began to gallop along with them. They, in order not to lose, could not protest or even laugh . . .

I shouted after them, "Platero's winning, Platero's winning!"

Yes, Platero reached the violets before anyone else and paused there to roll in the sand.

The children came back panting their protests, pulling up their stockings, pushing back their hair.

"That doesn't count! That doesn't count! No! No! Oh no!"

I told them that Platero had won the race and that it was only fair to give him some kind of prize. And anyway the book which Platero couldn't read would be left for another race of theirs but Platero must get a prize.

Now sure of the book, they jumped and laughed uproariously. "Yes, yes, yes!"

Then, thinking of myself, it seemed to me that Platero should have the first prize for his effort, I for my verses. And, taking a little parsley from the box at the door of the cottage, I made a crown and put it on his head, a fleeting first award like that won by a Lacedemonian.

11/DEATH

I found Platero stretched out on his bed of straw, his eyes soft and sad. I went to him, caressed him, talked to him and tried to get him up . . .

The poor thing moved jerkily and got up on one knee . . . He couldn't make it . . . then I stretched out his leg on the ground, caressed him again tenderly, and sent for his veterinary.

Old Darbon, when he saw him, opened his enormous toothless mouth from ear to ear and shook his red face like a pendulum above his chest.

"Not so good, eh?"

I don't know what he answered . . . that the poor animal was dying . . . that a pain . . . I don't know what poisonous root . . . the earth in the grass . . .

By midday Platero was dead. The little cottony belly was swollen like the world and his legs, rigid and discolored, were sticking upward. His curly hair looked like the motheaten tow on a doll's head which falls out in dusty sadness when you pass your hand over it.

In the silent stall, bursting into flame every time it passed through a ray of light from the little window, a beautiful tricolored butterfly circled about . . .

12/NOSTALGIA

Platero, you see us, don't you?

And you see, don't you, how the water of the well in the gar-

den laughs peacefully, clear and cool, as now in the late after-
noon light the industrious bees circle over the green and mallow-
pink rosemary, turned pink and gold by the sun still lighting up
the hilltop?

Platero, you see us, don't you?

You see, don't you, the little burros of the washerwomen pass-
ing over the red crest of the Old Fountain, tired, lame, sad, in
the immense purity that united earth and sky in a single crys-
tal of glory?

Platero, you see us, don't you?

You see, don't you, the children running suddenly between the
rock roses whose flowers, perched on their branches, are a frivol-
ous swarm of wandering white butterflies, spotted with carmine?

Platero, you see us, don't you?

Platero, it's true that you see us, isn't it? Yes, you see me. And
I think I hear you, yes, yes, I hear your gentle, plaintive bray in
the cloudless west, filling the valley of the vineyards with sweet-
ness . . .

13 / MELANCHOLY

This afternoon I have been with the children to visit the grave
of Platero which is in the Pine Orchard, at the foot of a thick,
paternal pine tree. Once again April had adorned the moist earth
with great yellow lilies.

The blue titmice were singing high up in the green tip, all
painted with azure sky, and their mute, florid, laughing, trill

pervaded the golden air of the warm afternoon like a clear dream of new love.

When we arrived the children stopped shouting. Quiet and serious, their shining eyes, fixed on mine, plied me with anxious questions.

"Platero, friend!" (I said to the earth), "If, as I think, you are now in the meadows of the sky and are carrying the adolescent angels on your furry back, have you perhaps forgotten me? Platero, tell me, do you still remember me?"

And, as if answering my question, another fragile white butter-fly, which I had not seen before, circled insistently from lily to lily, like a soul.

Platero y yo/1907-1916

3

1916-1925/ A new approach to poetry and prose

Madrid, Feb. 17, 1916

How close to the soul is all that
Which is still so immensely far
From our hands!
                              Like the light of a star,
Like a voice without a name,
Transmitted by dreams, like the distant tramp
Of some warhorse
That we strain to hear
With our ear to the ground,
Like the sea over a telephone . . .

And life is created within us
In the inextinguishable light

Of a delicious day
Shining somewhere else.

Oh how sweet, how sweet,
Truth, still without reality, how sweet!

Diario de un poeta recién casado/1916

February 1

You are all in yourself, sea, and yet
How much of you is not you, how lonely,
And forever far from yourself!
Open in a thousand wounds, each instant,
Like my forehead,
Like my thoughts your waves come and go,
And come and go,
Kissing withdrawing, sea,
In an eternal friendship
And estrangement.

You are you and do not know it,
Your heart beats and it does not feel it . . .
What a fulfillment of solitude, lonely sea!

Diario de un poeta recién casado/1916

NOCTURNE

February 3

Oh sea without familiar waves,
Without "stations" of rest,
Nothing but water and moon, nights and nights!

I remember the earth
Which, though distant, belonged to one,
Passing over it at night in trains
Through the same places and at the same times
As in other years.

Distant mother,
Sleeping earth
With firm and constant arms,
With the same quiet lap—
Tomb of eternal life—
With the same adornment renewed—
Mother earth, you who always
Retain in your single truth
The melancholy gaze
Of wandering eyes!

I remember the earth—
The olive trees at dawn—
Firm against the moon,
White, pink, or yellow,
Awaiting returns and returns
Of those who, without being her servants or masters
Loved her and loved her . . .

Diario de un poeta recién casado / 1916

SEA

It seems, sea, that you struggle—
Oh endless disorder, incessant weapon!
To reach yourself or that I may reach you.

What immense self-revelation, sea,
In your lonely nakedness—
Without a companion of either sex
According to whether I call you he or she—creating
The entire image
Of our world of today!

As if in childbirth you are bringing
Yourself into the world—with what weariness—
Into yourself, to yourself alone and in your own
And only abundance of abundances . . .
To reach yourself or that I may reach you!

Diario de un poeta recién casado/1916

SKY

February 7

I had forgotten you,
Sky, and you were no more
Than a vague presence of light,
Seen—nameless—
By my tired, indolent eyes.
And you appeared, among the lazy

And hopeless words of the traveler
As if in the brief repeated lagoons
Of a watery landscape seen in dreams . . .

Today I looked at you slowly
And you went on rising up to your name.

Diario de un poeta recién casado/1916

IDEAL ARRIVAL

February 11
To Joaquin Sorolla

Suddenly, a fan of gold, the evening opens like a great, real il-
lusion. With what a sense of well-being we are filled, with what
sweetness! It seems as if Turner has accompanied us. Seagulls
which we never noticed but which, no doubt, were there, make
their appearance, fly up beside the pennants on the mast, how
far from the sky but how high above us! The sky rises, departs,
vanishes, now it has no name, it is not a sky but a glory, a tran-
quil glory, still opal only, not yet turning to yellow. The sea
crinkles into a new shape and it seems that at the same time that
the sky rises more fluidly it descends, descends more liquidly.
Pieces of wood float by on the waves, barrels. We leave some fish-
ing boats behind . . . Have we arrived?

The setting sun tinges the port rail with pink, with nostalgic,
slanting rays. How joyous the red of the life preservers ignited
by the pink, how sweet the white of the rail ignited by the pink;
the black of this Negro woman, the olive of this Japanese; how
lovely all the eyes, the hair, the mouths in the setting sun! How
brotherly all of us are—black, white, and yellow—in this gaiety!

I listen with pleasure to the melancholy talk of this gentleman who takes opium, I answer the traveling salesman to whom I have not spoken all through the trip. I endure the friar's cigar smoke . . . imagination awakens, ignited in the faces. There is singing, dancing, no one wants to descend for dinner, faces are thrust into the new warmth which comes from the new world. To the starboard, along with our hopes, walk those who do not sing, or dream or love—

The moment is like a song rising from a dream and we are its heroes. Yes, we are the truth, the beauty, the eternal enduring strophe, captured by rhyme in the loveliest, half-glimpsed center of eternal poetry which we always know and are always hoping to know afresh—the second quatrain of a pure sonnet of the sea? Where are we? In what time do we exist? From what novel have we emerged? Are we an illustration? Have we arrived?

But the illustration fades and goes out. Never has an evening faded so completely! The sky descends again and the sea rises and they leave us as small as in daytime. Once more anxiety over time, the mist, cold noses, lack of space, the *petty things*. We who were talking a moment before, separate our silences. I walk along the canvas-covered, dripping rail. We go back to never arriving, to pushing time forward in our imagination, to sailing in two ships at the same time, to cursing the unchanging sea, the boring insipid sea, the eternal black marble streaked with white. Yes, marble on both sides of the clumsy ship, of this evil-smelling bear . . . my paper falls . . . I don't know what to write . . .

Diario de un poeta recién casado/1916

Birkendene, Caldwell
February, 20

I plucked off your petals as if you were a rose
In order to see your soul
And did not see it.

        But all about—
Horizons of earths and seas—
All, even to the infinite,
Was filled by an essence,
Immense and alive.

Diario de un poeta recién casado/1916

THE COLONIAL HOUSE

New York, March 26
To Aunt Bessie

What peace the old house, white and yellow as a daisy, of simple
wood and all closed up, collects in its ancient, dusty windows
with great mallow-pink panes, the gently slanting green and
pink setting sun of spring enriching, for a moment, the dark,
empty interior with light and color, with the image of the shore!
    It has been left alone on Riverside Drive, little and alone like
a clean little old man among the enormous, pretentious, and

ugly houses that surround it. It resembles a small shirt that has remained a tiny thing in the city. No one loves it. On its door a sign says: to let. And the joyful wind comes and plays with the card now and then so that it does not get bored.

But from its sepulchral solitude there emanates so much life force that a superimposition of lines and colors, its former countryside, fades and blurs and drives away the terrible masses of steel and stone which are choking it and creates around it a sweet, distant and solitary hill, green with long-expected rustic springtime, as it lies down softly on its side like a faithful dog, facing the river.

Diario de un poeta recién casado/1916

THE NEGRESS AND THE ROSE

New York, April 5
To Pedro Henríquez Ureña

The Negress is falling asleep with a white rose in her hand. *The rose and the dream dispel, in a magical superimposition, all the girl's sad finery: the pink openwork stockings, the transparent green blouse, the golden straw hat with the purple poppies.* In dreams defenseless, she smiles, the white rose in her black hand.

How tightly she holds it! It seems she is dreaming of clutching it carefully. Unconsciously she cares for it—with the precision of a somnambulist—and it is her own delicacy, as if this morning she had given birth to it, as if in dreams she felt herself to be the mother of a white rose's soul. *At times the crinkled nimbus, which would glisten in the sun if it were golden, nods on her breast or on her shoulder, but the hand which holds the rose defends its honor, standard bearer of spring.*

An invisible reality penetrates everything in the subway whose noisy, clashing blackness, both warm and dirty, is hardly felt. All have abandoned their newspapers, their gum, their cries, as in a nightmare of weariness and sadness they are absorbed in this white rose which the Negress glorifies, which is like the conscience of the subway. And the rose in the attentive silence emanates a delicious essence like a beautiful, immaterial presence which masters everything until iron and coal, the newspapers, all is for a moment perfumed by the white rose, by a better springtime, by eternity . . .

Diario de un poeta recién casado/1916

CEMETERY ON BROADWAY

New York, April 10
to Hannah Crooke

This tiny cemetery, open to the business section, is walled in by four rapid and constantly competing transportation systems: the elevated, the trolley, the taxi, and the subway, which never fail its obstinate, small silence. An endless glitter of fleeting reflections, with their counterparts, announces in gold and black letters all the *and Co.s* of New York in the shifting alchemy of the setting sun, collected interminably and variously as they meet, and strikes the backs and shoulders of the old tombstones whose blackened stone is tinged here and there with the color of the heart.

Poor pool of the dead with your toy church whose bells dream beside the offices which besiege your peace among the bells, the horns, the whistles, and the riveting hammers! . . . But the purity, little as it is, and embattled as it is, is infinite; and only the scanty, acid-green grass which the dead of another period bring forth, and the single little red flower which the slanting sun glorifies upon a tombstone fill with poetry this terrible hour of five o'clock and make the cemetery the only twin of the immense, transparent and silent sunset from whose endless beauty the living city is exiled.

Diario de un poeta recién casado/1916

THE MOON

New York, April 23
To Alfonso Reyes

Broadway. Evening. Signs in the sky that make one dizzy with color. New constellations: The Pig, all green, dancing and waving greetings to the left and right with his straw hat, the Bottle which pops its ruddy cork with a muted detonation against a sun with eyes and a mouth, the Electric Stocking which dances madly by itself like a tail separated from a salamander, the Scotchman who displays and pours his whiskey with its white reflections, the Fountain of mallow-pink and orange water through whose shower, like a snake, pass hills and valleys of wavering sun and shade, links of gold and iron (that braid a shower of light and another of darkness . . .), the Book which illuminates and extinguishes the successive imbecilities of its owner, the Ship which every moment, as it lights up, sails pitching toward its prison, to run aground immediately in the darkness . . . and . . .

The moon! Let's see! Look at it between those two tall buildings over there, above the river, over the red octave beneath,

don't you see it? Wait, let's see! No . . . is it the moon or just
an advertisement of the moon?

Diario de un poeta recién casado/1916

LONG LIVE SPRING

New York, the virago with dirty nails, wakes up. As the clear
stars at nightfall come surging into the light from darkness, so
do the black ships in the turbid Hudson, anchored in an iron
circle. Day is taking its place and picks up the telephone in its
Broadway office.

Springtime comes, with a desire for purity reinforced by the
dawn, swimming through the sky and water to the city. All
night she has been awake beautifying herself, bathing in the light
of the full moon. For a moment her roses, still warm, reflect the
beauty of the dawn which is struggling with the trust, "Smoke,
Shadow, Mud and Co.," which receives her with its pilot. But
alas the dawn falls back into the water almost defeated. Armies
of gold come in the sun to aid her. They draw her out dripping
and naked and give her artificial respiration in the Statue of
Liberty. The poor thing! How delighted she is, still timid though
conquering!

The pale gold of nine o'clock is enough to make her a queen.
Yes, the dirty buds on the trees on the piers smile with a blond
grace; the sparrows on the fire escapes sing matters of gold, still
black with memories of snow, the cemeteries on the shores ex-
plode the soot into thin sparks, a pink band in the east enchants

the signs on the towers, bells of fire alarms and all the church bells ring in confusion . . .

Behold her! She is here now, naked and strong in Washington Square, beneath the arch, ready to march up Fifth Avenue toward the park, her naked thighs already begin to mark time, without moving forward. She bends her head. Now!

Long live spring! Long live spring! Long live spring!

Diario de un poeta recién casado/1916

NOCTURNE

For Antonio Machado

. . . It is the celestial geometry
Of an old astronomer
Above the tall city—towers,
Dark, slender, small, termination of this . . .
As if from an ultimate observatory
The astronomer
Were looking at it.

Precise
Signs—fires and colors—
With their secret spread out underneath
In a diaphanous atmosphere
Of deep blue transparency.

What brilliance, what menace,
What insistence, what prophecies,
In the immanent certitude

Of strange truth! Anatomy
Of the sky, the science
Of its movement within it and for us!

A sharp cry, immense and lonely—
Like a falling star—
                    How far
From what we were,
From that spring afternoon yesterday—
In serene and pleasant Washington Square—
From those dreams and that love!

Diario de un poeta recién casado/1916

CEMETERIES

*Between New York and Philadelphia
May 19*

Once again yes. A hundred times! For me the greatest attraction of America lies in the charm of its cemeteries. Unwalled, near to us they seem the true poetic city of each city attracting us with their agreeable and bird-chanted peace, more in the midst of life than the parks, the ports, the museums . . . a little girl walks from her house to another between the gravestones, blue and violet beneath the green, stopping absent-mindedly to play with her doll or to follow a butterfly with her eyes. The crosses are reflected in the ivy-hung windowpanes of the next houses, in the cool peace created by an atmosphere which relates house and grave in the same shadow. The birds of the moment fly from the cross to the window, as tranquil among the living as is the girl on the hill among the dead.

What a triumph here of beauty over death, a welcome and peaceful example in the midst of so many evil examples of haste and disorder. Oh rose well savored, Oh water well drunk, Oh dream well dreamed! How well the dead must rest among you, familiar hills of New York, bright with eternal life in the midst of the life of every day!

Diario de un poeta recién casado/1916

EVENING

At the pier now in the red and opal evening,
In the weeping wind of this evening,
By turns warm and cool,
The black ship is waiting.

Tonight we will still turn to
What is already almost nothing—
To where all is being left behind
Without us—
Disloyal to what is ours.
And the black ship is waiting—

We say: everything is ready!
And our eyes turn sadly back
Seeking something we do not know which is no more with us,
Something we have not seen,
Which has not been ours,
But is ours because it might have been!

Good-by! Good-by! Good-by! To everywhere, though we have
   not yet gone,
And, not wanting to, are almost going!

All is left behind with its life,
Left behind without ours.
Good-by from tomorrow—now we are homeless—
To you and in you, unknown you, to myself even,
To you who never reached me, even though you were running,
To you whom I never reached, even though I hurried—
How sad the space between us!

. . . And, seated, we weep, still without going,
And, already far away, we weep with eyes
Against the wind and sun which are struggling crazily.

Diario de un poeta recién casado / 1916

INTELLIGENCE

Intelligence, give me
The exact name of things!
Let my word be
The thing itself,
Newly created by my soul.
Through me may all those
Who have no knowledge of things reach them;
Through me may all those
Who have forgotten things reach them;

Through me may all those
Who even love things reach them . . .
Intelligence, give me
The exact name, and yours,
And his, and mine, of things!

Eternidades/1916-1917

POETRY

When first she came to me chastely,
Dressed in her innocence only,
As a little girl I loved her truly.

Then she took to adorning herself
With all sorts of finery
And I hated her not knowing why.

At last she became a queen,
Gaudily hung with jewelry . . .
What bitter contrariness and how senseless!

But once more she began undressing
And I smiled upon her.

She was left in her slip,
Her former innocence.
And again I believed in her.

And she took off her slip, too,
And appeared quite naked . . .
Oh naked poetry, my lifelong passion,
Now you are mine forever!

Eternidades/1916-1917

To the bridge of love,
Old stone between high rocks—
Eternal rendezvous, red afternoon—
I come with my heart.

My beloved is none but the water,
Always flowing and never deceiving;
Always flowing and never changing,
Always flowing and never ending.

Eternidades/1916-1917

Sleep is like a bridge   .
Which reaches from today to tomorrow.

84

Below, like a dream,
The water flows by.

Eternidades/1916-1917

How strange
The two of us and our instinct!
Suddenly we are four.

Eternidades/1916-1917

I recognized you because when I saw the print
Of your foot on the pathway
My heart hurt when you trod upon me.
I ran madly; I went seeking all day long
Like a dog without a master.
You were gone already! And your foot was treading
On my heart, in an endless flight
As if this were the roadway
That carried you off forever . . .

Eternidades/1916-1917

Don't run, go slowly,
It is only to yourself that you have to go!

Go slowly, don't run,
For the child of yourself, just born
And eternal
Cannot follow you.

Eternidades/1916-1917

Every poplar, as you pass it,
Sings a moment in the wind
Which is in it, and each one, at that moment—
Love—is the oblivion
And the memory of the other.

It is just one poplar—love—
That is singing.

Eternidades/1916-1917

DEAD

His weight remains constant:
One pan of the scale in the mud,
One pan in the sky.

Eternidades/1916-1917

(To Miss Rápida)

If you hurry so,
Time will fly ahead of you like a
Fleeing butterfly.

If you go slowly,
Time will walk behind you
Like a submissive ox.

Eternidades/1916-1917

I am not I.
            I am he,
Who walks at my side without my seeing him,

Who at times I am about to see,
Who, at times, I forget.
He, who is silent, serene when I am speaking;
He, who pardons gently when I am hating;
He, who walks where I am not,
He, who shall stand erect when I am dead.

Eternidades/1916-1917

I am like a distracted child
Whom they drag by the hand
Through the fiesta of the world.
My eyes cling, sadly,
To things . . .
And what misery when they tear me away from them!

Eternidades/1916-1917

THE POEM

I

Do not touch it any more
For that is how a rose is!

88

2

Pull the plant up by the roots,
Still full of the dew of sunrise.

Oh what a watering
Of the fragrant, moist earth,
What a rain—what a blindness—
From bright stars on my forehead, in my eyes!

Piedra y cielo/1917-1918

TO BELOVED OLD AGE

Alas, if your memory
Of me were this blue May sky
All filled
With the spotless stars of my actions!
With my actions like them, all spotless,
Clean, good, tranquil, like the stars.
Below, your smile in dreams—
Dreams of your memories of my life!

Piedra y cielo/1917-1918

SEAS

I feel that my vessel has struck
Down in the depths
Upon some huge thing.

And nothing
Happens! Nothing . . . quiet . . . waves . . .

Nothing happens, or has everything happened
And we are already tranquilly in the new?

Piedra y cielo/1917-1918

NOCTURNE OF DREAMS

The earth takes us through the earth
But you, sea,
Take us through the sky,
With what assurance of silver and gold light
The stars mark out
The route for us . . . one would say
The earth is the pathway
Of the body,
The sea is the highway
Of the soul.
Yes, it seems
That the soul is the only voyager
On the sea, the body alone

Is left behind on the beaches,
Without her, having said farewell,
Heavy, cold, as if dead.
How similar
Sea voyage is to the voyage of death,
The voyage of eternal life!

Nostaljía del mar / 1917-1918

IDEAL EPITAPH FOR A SAILOR

One must look through the firmament
To find your tomb.
Your death rains down from a star.
The stone does not oppress you, it is a universe
Of dream.
In ignorance you exist
In everything—sky, sea, and earth—dead.

Piedra y cielo / 1917-1918

SONG

All of autumn, rose,
Is this single one of your petals
Falling.

Girl, all of sorrow
Is this single drop
Of your blood.

Piedra y cielo/1917-1918

Yes—says day—no—
Says night.

Who will pluck off the petals of this immense daisy
Of gold, white, and black?

And tell us when, Lord of the uncreated,
You will believe that we love you?

Piedra y cielo/1917-1918

AROUND THE TIP

Around the tip
Of a tall tree
My dreams are flying.

They are doves crowned with
Pure lightrays
And as they fly they scatter music.

What a going and coming
From a single treetip!
How they enmesh me in gold!

UNVEILING

A black bull, the night departs—
All somber flesh, full of fear and mystery;
It has bellowed frightfully, immensely,
To the sweating terror of all the fallen;
And the day comes, an unsullied child,
Seeking trustfulness, love, and laughter—
A child which far, far away,
In the secret recesses
Where beginnings and ends meet,
Was playing for a moment
In some unknown meadow
Of light and shadow
With the bull that fled.

93

LIGHT AND WATER

The light above—golden, orange, green—
Among the misty clouds.

Oh trees without leaves,
Rooted in water,
Branching in the light!

Below, the water—green, orange, golden—
Among the misty vapors.

Among the misty vapors, among the misty clouds,
Light and water—what magics!—vanish.

Poesía/1917-1923

Leave the doors open
Tonight lest he,
Who is dead should wish
To come in tonight.
            Everything open
To see if we resemble
His body, to see if we
Are some part of his soul, being
Surrendered to space,
To see if the great infinite
Will lift us, by invading us,

A little out of ourselves: if we die
A little here, there, in him,
We live a little.
                    Open
All the house, just as if
The body were present
In the blue night,
With us like our own blood,
With the stars for flowers!

Poesía/1917-1923

DAWNS OF MOGUER

The silver elm trees
Emerging from the mist!
The solitary wind
Moving through the dusky
Swampland—unreal
Earthquake—the diffuse
And distant pink town of Huelva!
Above the sea, by the Rábida
In the grey-pearled moisture
Of the sky still cold from
The night, through a harsh dawn—
Horizon of pine trees—
Cold through the white dawn,
The dazzled moon!

Poesía/1917-1923

MY VOICE

Sing, sing, voice of mine,
While there is something
You have not yet said.
You have said nothing at all.

Poesía/1917-1923

THIS IS MY LIFE

This is my life: what is high above,
What exists in pure breeze,
In the ultimate bird,
In the golden summits of darkness!

This is my liberty: smelling the rose,
Cutting the cold water with my crazy hand,
Plucking the grove bare,
Snatching the sun's eternal light!

Poesía/1917-1923

DEATH

The little strength you still had
You spent in two last smiles,
You still offered them to me. Then
You ceased.
Against your will serious forever.

Poesía/1917-1923

THE WATCHER

My eyes wide open!
Carry me to the sea,
To see if I am sleeping.

While they may be far from it,
They will never be closed,
My wide open eyes.

They will weep memories
Until they make a sea
Of weeping and desire.

A comfortless sea
Which must carry me
To eternal wakefulness.

Neither kisses nor sweet singing
Can imitate
The wind and the waves.

The wind and the waves!
Carry me to the sea,
To see if I am sleeping.

THE ONLY FRIEND

You will not reach me, friend.
You will arrive, anxious, crazy,
But I shall have already gone.

And what a fearful emptiness,
All that you have left behind
To come to me!

And what a wretched abyss,
All that I have placed
Between, without meaning to, friend!

You can not remain, friend . . .
Perhaps I shall return to the world
But you will have already gone.

98

SOUTH

Sharp nostalgia, infinite
And terrible, for what I already possess!

Poesía/1917-1923

THE LITTLE GREEN BIRD

I have come here.
But I left my weeping there.
At the shore of the sea,
Weeping.

I have come here.
But I can be of no use to you
Because I left my soul
There.

I have come here.
But you may not call me brother,
For my soul is there,
Weeping.

Poesía/1917-1923

They shall not stare at me saying,
"What are you?"
Except incuriously
And gently.

Because I, too, shall be
Of the quiet ones,
And now I shall not have
Difficult thoughts.

My eyes will be serene,
Theirs;
I shall stare at them without questions,
One in the one.

Poesía/1917-1923

THE WATER IN THE WATER

I should like my life
To fall into death

Like this tall stream of lovely water,
In the supine water of the morning,
Rippling, brilliant, sensual, joyful,
With all of the world dissolved in it
In gay and shining grace.

Belleza/1917-1923

THE LIE

Now they lie buried together.
Ah, what a cold, twin secret!
Not their secret of death—
Less ugly, less grey than
Their secret of living.
(What double deception in sunlight!)

Shriveled now, will they never
Trustfully tell each other?
Are they alone forevermore,
Venom of sad roses,
Accursed stone usurping
The earth that once made them?

Lying fragrance, flowers
Of their hearts! False mineral
Of their wilfulness!

Is the anguish now, the decomposed
Sadness of their having been alive

Pulsating still in the world,
Since what was will be eternal
Suffocation, keeping them buried
With its "now irrevocable"?

And will they never return
In springtime, for an instant
Of love, yearning to tell each other?

Belleza/1917-1923

WHITE ELM TREE

High above the bird is singing
And below the water is singing.
Above and below
My soul is opening.

Between two melodies,
The column of silver!
Leaves, bird, star,
Twig, roots, water.

Between two commotions,
The column of silver!
And you, ideal tree-trunk,
Between my soul and my soul!

The star cradles the trill,
The wave the low hanging branch.

Above and below
My soul is trembling.

I SHOULD LIKE TO SLEEP DURING THIS NIGHT

I should like to sleep during this night
That you lie dead, to sleep,
To sleep, to sleep alongside
The completeness of your sleep,
To see if this way I can reach you!

To sleep, a sunrise at evening,
Source of the river, to sleep;
Two days that gleam together
In nothingness, two currents
Flowing, together at the end;
Two alls if this is anything,
Two nothings if all is nothing.

I should like to sleep your death!

ZENITH

I shall not be I, O death,
Until you come to join my life
And so make me entirely whole;
Until my half of light is locked
Into my half of shadow.
Thus I may be forever balanced
Within the world's mind,
At times the half of me aglow,
At times the half of me oblivion—

I shall not be I, O death,
Until you, in your turn,
Shall dress my soul in these pale bones.

Belleza/1917-1923

4

1925-1936/From the years of maturity in rhythm and thought

GENERALIFE*

(To Isabelita García Lorca, little fairy of the Generalife.)

No one else. All open.
But then no one was missing.
They were not women or children,
They were not men, they were tears—
Who could carry the immensity
Of their tears—
Which were trembling, flowing,
Throwing themselves in the water?

* In Granada, the gardens of the summer palace of the last Moorish king, notable for their fountains.

The waters were talking, weeping,
Under the white rosebays,
Under the red rosebays,
The waters were weeping, singing,
By the flowering myrtle,
Above the opaque waters.

Madness of singing and weeping,
Of souls and of tears!
Between four walls
The waters suffer like flames:
Souls are talking and weeping
Tears forgotten,
The waters are singing, weeping
Cloistered souls.

Yonder they are killing her!
Yonder they are bearing her off!
She is seen naked—
Run, run, they are fleeing!
And the soul wants to go out
And to change into a handful of water,
To run everywhere
With a flood of words,
To turn into a suffering tear,
In the waters, with the souls . . .
Up the stairs!
No, they descend the staircase!
What a frightful confusion
Of souls, waters, and tears,
What a pale heaping up
Of frantic flights!
And who knows what they desire?

Where to kiss? Soul, how to see
Not souls and not tears
Quivering in the water?
They can not be separated;
Let them fly, let them go!
Have they gone to smell the magnolias,
To peep out through the walls,
To hide in the cypress,
To speak to the fountain below?
Silence, now they weep no more!
Listen, now they speak no more!
The water is sleeping and dreaming
They are sweeping away its tears,
The souls it possessed
Were not tears but wings;
Sweet little girl in her garden,
Woman with her scarlet rose,
Child who stared at the world,
Man with his betrothed . . .
That it was singing and laughing . . .
That it was singing and weeping
With the reds of the setting sun,
In the tallest tears,
In the loudest cries,
To wander with bleeding soul!

Languid, supine, broken,
The white and heavenly water!
How disjointedly
She raises herself on her arms!
She speaks with more faith to her dreams
Which vanish from her anxieties;
It seems that she resigns herself

Giving her hand to the soul,
While the star of that time,
Eternal presence, deceives her.

But now she returns once more
To the direction of her misfortune;
She puts her face in her hands,
Wanting no one and nothing,
And begging to die,
And flying without any hope.
The waters are talking, weeping,
The souls are weeping, singing.
Oh what a disconsolate waste
Of fetching and carrying,
What an arrival at the last corner
In sleepwalking repetition;
What a beating of the head
Against the ultimate walls!

The soul is lost in water
And the body sinks down without soul,
The body departs without tears
Which it leaves behind with the water,
Weeping, talking, singing—
With the souls, with the tears
Of the labyrinth of suffering—
Among the white rosebays,
Among the pink rosebays
Of the brown and silver evening
With the myrtle now turning black
Beneath the closed in fountains.

Unidad / 1925

MADRID WIND

Gusts. Coming and going. The sky opens and shuts, blue, white, and leaden, with blindly explosive knives of gold and silver, in a constant furious fantasy of light. Above the city in intermittent shadow, rather cold, melancholy touches of trembling sunlight, high up on the lightningrods, on a muffled face that peers out of a garret to get something, on the twisted chimneys, on the hanging clothes which make the city into a ship, on the wires, on some forgotten flowerpot, humble with weak, martyred greenery.

It seems as if the wind has taken on flesh and approaches the human; a body drunk with space, goes stumbling over the earth, happy, blinded, sad, in the thousand forms of its vinous delirium. It careers suddenly and terrifying upward, it whirls downward, it spreads out and does not fit, it shakes closed houses, howls, laughs, weeps, sings infinite notes, at the same time clings to corners, beats women, plunges into miserable, cobbled alleys, maltreating, abusing everything that is delicate in life.

Distant horizons, level and quiet between the cubes of sun and shade formed by agitated houses, become pure, open, ideal—solid forgotten seas rained with changeable color at intervals—with broad, stationary, parallel bands of cloud, stretched like great cranes flying in the distance, immensely immobile.

Unidad/1925

DEPARTURE

(Purity of the Sea)

Until those pure nights of yours, sea,
My soul—more lonely than ever—did not feel

That desire to set out on some appointed day,
Unreasoning.
That gateway,
On the road the moon sets alight in you
With all the beauty of its centuries
Of chastity, whiteness, peace, and grace,
Is tinged with the yearning of its absent
Movement.
Frothing
With souls of lilies that a celestial music
Was creating from liquid crystals
On rods of hyaline summits of waves,
Colors exactly matched
To a sharp aroma of delights
That fill life with ecstasy until death.

Magic, delight, still more, in the shadow
Where those brilliant, staring eyes burn,
Than the vision of that hymned love,
Light, simple, true,
That we do not expect to attain, so certainly
Did it resemble the most distant dream!
Yes indeed, so it was, so it began;
That was how my child's heart
Viewed it when my eyes,
Opening like roses,
Were raised darkly from those towers
Of my dream, set shining by the rainbow,
To the loft clarity of a paradise!
And so there was that petal of sky
In which my soul found itself
The same as in another self, unique and free!
That was, this is, the place from which it went on

Through smooth galleries of infallible
Architectures of water, land, fire, and air,
Like this eternal night, to I know not where
In the sure light of a few stars.
So began the endless beginning,
Morning desire of my soul
To go out through its door toward its unknown center!

Oh primal whiteness, only and always
Primal!
Marble reality of unconscious, white lustre!
Mad whiteness, not to be repeated!
Whiteness of this night, sea, of moonlight!

Unidad / 1925

THE SOLITARY POPLAR

I already saw it in my profound adolescent dreams, bent over like
an indomitable arc of fire by a great vehement autumn twilight
wind—one of those short, acid-green solitary trees that rise to the
zenith in deaf negation; like a prodigious meteor of the evening
—a sudden secret martyr, rooted only in its errant mystery,
uselessly scattering its beautiful sparks, drops of red light, divine
golden leaves, in the torment of high solitude.

Terrible, sad, ardent, solitary Spanish poplar.

Unidad / 1925

FINAL AUTUMN

Among the diffuse, thin, grey foliage of La Castellana, tinged, by an occasional pine tree, with a dark, round mass of vivid green, great sycamore leaves still continue obstinately to hang here and there which the struggling sun of one o'clock, opening and closing among the ragged emerald crystals of the sky, sets afire with iridescent gold or extinguishes in clear yellow.

Some children, their smooth cheeks already blue, wearing mufflers, berets, leggings and gloves, schoolbags on their backs, trot by to school—in S curves and angles around benches and trees. A vendor of paper pinwheels goes along staining the tranquil silver vagueness of the early afternoon with his violent fan of red, yellow, green, and purple.

A beautiful woman, effete with wealth and refinement, extraordinarily white in a complete costume of black velvet, comes slowly down the tiled walk, at this hour of dinner almost deserted. She stops a moment, pulls out a little mirror, and looks at herself. She goes on again more slowly; she hesitates, she fixes her radiant leonine eyes on the restless south . . . once more she takes out the little mirror and looks at herself . . .

Unidad/1925

SEA, NOTHING

Sad rainclouds
Cast shadows on the sea.
                    The water

Stained like iron,
Seems like a hard level plain
Of exhausted mines,
In some ruin
Of flowing slag,
Of liquid destruction.

What a rising and falling, what a shuffle,
What a putting and taking
Of dark desolate planes!

A sea without virtue of sea, a useless sea
Without sea, a lost sea,
A sea of the past and forgetfulness,
A black sea of nothing,
Of accumulated furious nothing.

Nothing!
            Today, for me,
The word finds its place
In a rigid catastrophe,
Like the corpse of a word
Which should be stretched out in its natural
Sepulchre.
            Nothing and sea!

Unidad/1925

NEW SPRING

In the red water
Two swans swam side by side . . .
Pain swam in my blood.

In the red wind
Two roses yearned side by side . . .
Pain yearned in my blood.

In the red sky
Two blackbirds whistled side by side . . .
Pain whistled in my blood.

Canción/1935

WESTERN MOON

Back of my forehead I feel tonight
A whole sky full of stars.
Under a western moon
Life is indeed lovely!

The distant belltowers,
The swaying copses,
(And unknown white hands
Are caressing our lives)
The garden awakening
And sleeping, the song of

The fountain, the vigilant folksong
The heart never forgets,
And the shadow that grows,
And the roses exuding
A blue fragrance that seems
Exalted by the moonlight.

And the garden . . . all the stars . . .
I could swear it is true
That I lie dead . . . the lovely moon
Dies above the city.

Canción / 1935

SEPULCHRAL NIGHT

This horrible coldness
That fills the dead with delight
And overwhelms the living!

A terrible fire
That may madden the living
And consume the dead!

Canción / 1935

MY GREEN GARDEN

Green garden, I tend you
With the love in this song:
You shall never know oblivion,
Garden of my heart!

Is the time of weeping upon us?
You shall not think of dying,
For the strength of my great love
Shall sustain your living.
Think no more of dying!

(And garden, hear, when that miser,
The sun, guards his shifting gold,
You shall see it is clear and burning,
Matutinal, overflowing.

If the cloudy zenith should drench you,
I shall open my red arteries
And I shall melt the snowflakes
In the palms of your leaves.)

And should you know some morning
What a night of winter means,
Garden you shall not perish,
Your rebirth shall be eternal,
Garden that shall never die!

You shall flourish forever,
Warm in my passion's fire:
You shall not know oblivion,
Garden of my heart!

Canción / 1935

MOST MINE

I cannot tell myself why
You hold me back.
I do not know what the matter is.

You have lived sweet years
But they are not your years;
You are exceedingly white
But it is not your whiteness;
You have a lofty forehead
But it is not your forehead;
You have green hair
But it is not your hair;
You have golden eyes,
You have living lips
But they are not your eyes,
But they are not your lips;
You are full of harmony,
It is not your melody;
You are full of spleen,
It is not your heart . . .

I cannot tell you why
You hold me back.
I do not know what the matter is . . .

Canción / 1935

PRELUDE TO AUTUMN

In the open window I await you, autumn. Come
And cool my temples
With the spreading fragrance
Of a withered rose.

The early morning hour is lost in shadow. And all things
Come to an end in another way.
And love magnifies itself in an intense pulsation,
A huge journeying.

Life is farther away. The intimate landscape
Plaits foam and lace.
And yonder, where the tranquil branches leave spaces,
Sublime circles
Bury themselves within.

       And the sweetness is wandering and unquiet.
And a vivid coolness
Arises from the soil . . . autumn I grow impatient. Come
And caress my temples.

Canción / 1935

BIRD OF THE WATER

Bird of the water,
You are chanting what enchantment?

To the early evening
You give a nostalgia
Of eternal coolness,
Of moistened glory.
The sun disrobes
Above your cantata.

Bird of the water!

From the rosebushes
Of my garden it is calling
To those lovely clouds
Laden with tears.
It would like to see drops of
Silver on the roses.

Bird of the water!

My song, too,
Is a song of water.
In my springtime
The grey clouds float down
To the rosebushes
Of my hopes.

Bird of the water!

I love the wandering
Blue sound you unstring like beads
Upon the green leaves,
Upon the white fountain.
Do not leave me,
Heart with wings!

Bird of the water,
What enchantment are you chanting?

Canción/1935

THE ROSEMARY FLOWER

(For me bellowing shall hold
Greater delights
Than hearing nightingales.
                              —Santilla)

Yesterday you were alone
Among the rosemary flowers
Would that the sand would permit me to meet you
To tell you I love you.

Queen of the field, grant me a moment
Full of peace and forgetfulness.
Woman of moon and sun, shepherdess,
Will you watch over my life?

Yesterday you were alone
Among the rosemary flowers . . .

If but your blue glances could give me
Rosemary flowers for my soul!
Oh to graze on the flower on your hillside
In twilights of calm!

Yesterday you were alone
Among the rosemary flowers . . .

The morning-glory of my life
Is a tear. And as long as it grazes
From flower to flower and forgets,
My tears shall be turned to music.

Yesterday you were alone
Among the rosemary flowers . . .

Afternoon and morning sun!
Solitude, powerful plant!
Rosemary flower, and soul, sound
Against the dark shadow of death!

Yesterday you were alone
Among the rosemary flowers,
Would today the road would permit me to meet you
To tell you that I love you.

Canción/1935

THE MOON IN THE PINE TREE

The moon was in the pine tree,
Pink in the violet heaven.
Now the pine tree comes by in a wagon,
Dead and soundless.

Will the moon come into the pine tree?

Over the dust of the roadway
There is that violet sweetness,
Will the sky bring it down, wagon,
To its moon here in the roadway?

Does the moon go by in the pine tree?

How sadly the pine tree passes
Brushing the violet ground!
The wagon weeps with light,
Weeps with verdure for the pine tree.

Does the moon weep in the pine tree?

Where is the divine lily
Born lonely and violet?
The wagon carries pinkness
Like a divine effulgence!

Is the moon in the pine tree?

The moon was in the pine tree,
Pink in the violet heaven,
Now it comes by in a wagon,
Dead and soundless, the pine tree.

Does the moon go by in the pine tree?

Canción/1935

THE ROCKROSE

(Berthe aux sages yeux de lilas,
qui priais que je revinses,
que fais-tu, mariée la-bas, en province?
                                    —Laforgue.)

Wear white, life, at seeing
The rockrose on the mountain.

Rockrose, flowering today,
White, spotted with carmine,
How often I have remembered you
Among the roses in my garden.

Wear white, sorrow, at seeing
The rockrose on the mountain.

Happy vigorous butterfly!
(You entered into my darkness,
You lit upon everything
And drew the truth out of it,)

Wear white, shadow, at seeing
The rockrose on the mountain.

You were dawn and delight,
You were peace and song;
What filled full of harmony
The solitude of the heart.

Wear white, illusion, at seeing
The rockrose on the mountain.

Today you live again, mountain,
To show me the heaven I have lost.

Oh lie to me, lie to me, rockrose,
And say you are really mine!

Wear white, dream, at seeing
The rockrose on the mountain.

Canción / 1935

THE WILD BIRD

Sing, distant bird . . .
(In what garden, in what meadow?)

Meanwhile shall I not arise?
In the room's penumbra
The closed piano is shining,
The dim pictures are gleaming . . .

For me, distant bird.

There will be above the river
A mirrored west of a thousand enchantments,
A gay vessel will leap out
Between the light of the elm trees . . .

Sing, distant bird.

In the orchard, the orange trees
Will be swollen with birds,

The blue will go singing
In the water of the rivulet . . .

For me, distant bird.

You, pinewood, deep palace,
You will catch at the placid wind,
The sea will enter billowing
Among the white rosebays . . .

Sing, distant bird.
I can not make up my mind, I wander
About in the room's penumbra.
The closed piano is humming,
The dim pictures are living . . .

For me, distant bird . . .
(In what rosebush, in what treetop?)

Canción / 1935

SWEET MARJORAM OF THE FOUNTAIN

(Smiling dream)

I went singing . . . the white, sad moonlight
Was turning the hill into something fearful.
Then you, baker, made your appearance
White with moonlight, spikenard, and flour.

Sweet marjoram of the mountain,
You were white with moonlight, sweet marjoram.

"Tell me, what do you seek?" "I gather moonlight
Among the sweet marjoram on the hill.
I long to be whiter than anyone,
Whiter than Rocío, Estrella, Francina."

Sweet marjoram of the mountain,
You were white with moonlight, sweet marjoram.

"You are whiter than the lowest bright star,
Whiter than the dew, the star, and the flour.
Your arms light up the pathway
That goes whitely down the hillside."

Sweet marjoram of the mountain,
You were white with moonlight, sweet marjoram.

Then you took me in your arms, baker,
White with starlight and with flour.
Dawn was breaking, the sad, pink moon
Went off leaving sunrise on the hilltop.
Sweet marjoram of the mountain,
You were pink with moonlight, sweet marjoram.

Canción / 1935

BLACK HAIR

I

Past my garden of flesh and moonlight,
Proud and bitter black hair went by.

The night was deadly, the full moon lived
Within itself, warm and supreme.

All secrets were out in the open air,
Gleaming at their god, enjoying the coolness.

What a catastrophe of roses and kisses,
What a flight from invading hair!

And from the sky my moon was shooting
Silver arrows against the black hair!

2

It laid waste my garden. The iron
Of its threads mowed down my thoughts.

No stalk of light was left, not a dream
In the place of its eternal ecstasy.

And in the concave steely west
Black hair stood quite still.

In the morning everyone said to me,
"How the wind has ravaged your garden!"

But still in my heart the fury was whistling
Of the hurricane of black hair.

Canción/1935

MOGUER NOCTURNE

The trees are not alone
For their shadows are with them.
But the soul is quite alone.

Into the valley the moon tosses
Its whole circle of silver.
The mad star flowers,
A vineyard of ashes.

The hills do not walk alone
For their breezes walk with them.
But the soul walks quite alone.

One can hear the world whistling,
Conch shells accompany it,
The sea goes thieving
In the round embrace of man and woman.

And the rivers do not flow alone,
For their waves flow with them.
But the soul flows quite alone.

Canción/1935

ATMOSPHERE

They were closing the doors
Against the tempest.

In the hurrying sky
Between two reports,
Showering javelins
From the anvil of the west,
The lightning opened
Tragic infinities.

They were closing the doors
Against the tempest.

All were hiding,
Waxen faces
Green from angers,
The unmoving apocalyptic
Cloud was filtering
Through the crevices.

They were closing the doors
Against the tempest.

But you were going naked,
Your flesh of moonlight
In the dark cloud,
Through the flashes—
Oh what architectures—
Ultimate terraces!

They were closing the doors
Against the tempest.

Canción/1935

THE LITTLE GREEN GIRL

The girl is green. She possesses
Eyes of green, hair of green.

Her woodland rosebud
Is not pink nor white but green.

She comes in the green air!
The earth turns green.

Her bright gauzy dress
Is neither white nor blue but green.

She comes in the green sea!
The sky turns green.

My life continually opens
A little door of green for her.

Canción/1935

THE FIRST

White within the blue.
And the night. And you.

You return with the night
From your youth

To my lonely garden
Where you never appear
In the blue daylight.

White within the shadow.
And the white. And you.

You return dim and white
To my youth
Beneath the green tree
Where you never appear
In the blue daylight.

White within the blue.
And whiter. And you.

Canción / 1935

THE ETERNAL DAMSEL

The eternal damsel
Returns with the moon,
Every springtime.

Flowers surround her,
Lustreless and serene,
In graceful flight.

(Every springtime
The eternal damsel
Returns with the breeze),

Flowers, both human
And celestial, mingle
In her virgin life.

(The eternal damsel
Returns with the river
Every springtime),

Clouds of honeysuckle,
Bright star of jasmine,
Star of lily.

Every springtime
The eternal damsel
Returns with the soul.

Canción/ 1935

THE ONE BEING

Let nothing invade me from without
That I may listen to my inner self only.
I, god
Of my breast.

(I everything: sunset and sunrise,
Love, friendship, life and dream.

I, alone
Universe.)

Pass by, do not think of my life,
Leave me slender and submerged.
I, one
In the midst of myself.

Canción / 1935

ULTIMATE ROSE

Gather it, gather the rose!
But no, it is the sun!

The rose of flame,
The rose of gold,
The ideal rose.

But no, it is the sun!

The rose of glory,
The rose of dreams,
The final rose.

But no, it is the sun!
Gather it, gather the rose!

Canción / 1935

THE GARDENER OF SEVILLE

In Seville, in Triana, in a handsome garden above the Guadal-
quivir River, on Nightingale Street, too (this seems too much but
such coincidences are authentically of the people), from a patio
the sun can be seen setting against the cathedral and La Giralda,
tips of pink flame in the dark green. The market gardener, a big,
sensitive man, sold plants and flowers that he raised with ex-
quisitely painstaking care in his greenhouse. He loved every
plant and flower as if they were women or delicate children; this
was a family of leaves and flowers. And what it cost him to sell
them, to let them go, to deprive himself of them! This spiritual
conflict (and it took place daily) went on over a potful of hy-
drangeas.

Some people came to buy it and he, after thinking it over and
hesitating a long time, finally compromised on certain condi-
tions. He would sell it but on condition, he insisted, that he
watch over it. The hydrangea bush was taken away. For some
days the gardener went to look at it in the house of the new
owners. He took off the dead leaves, he watered it, he put in or
took out a little earth, he arranged the stalks. And before he left
he lingered a while to give instructions for its care. "It must be
watered this way and not that way, it must only get the sun
this way, and be very careful, Madam, about the dew, too
much here, too much there."

The owners began to tire of his visits ("Fine, fine, my good
man. Don't worry. Until next month, etc.") and so the gardener
came less often, that is, he came anyway but he did not go in.
He passed through the street and looked at the hydrangea bush
through the front door. Or he entered quickly, covering his em-
barrassment with the pretext, "I've brought a spray that I picked
up so that you can water it better," or, "I forgot this piece of wire
netting," or some other such excuse. And with these excuses he
got to "his" hydrangea bush.

Finally, one day he came again and announced, "If you don't
want me to come and look after it, tell me what I owe you for
it, because I'm taking it back to my house now." And he
clutched the blue pot full of pink hydrangeas in his arms as if it
had been a girl and took it away.

Verso y prosa para niños/1936

LISTENING TO THE WATER

As it grew dark, I was sitting by the lonely little Staircase of
Water in Generalife, in Granada, weary from the pleasures of an
afternoon of successive paradisal delights, sunk in a weightless
shadow, without substance, in the great growing shadow which
was turning dark yet was all shot through with celestial trans-
parency, leaving the stars naked in their places.

The water surrounded me with sounds of color and a supreme
coolness, near and far off, arising from all of its channels, all of
its showers and streams. As I was seated by it, the water fell
endlessly, close to my ears which caught the finest murmur
which had the affective quality of an exquisite and marvelously
harmonious instrument, or rather, absorbed in itself, was no
longer an instrument but a music of water, music made into
water, in turn and interminably. And I heard that music of water
both more and less clearly at the same time, less because it was
now no longer outside me but intimately mine; the water was
my blood, my life and I heard the music of my life and my blood
in the flowing water. Through the water I communicated with
the interior of the world. The water could be heard more dis-

tinctly; the darker the air grew, the louder the water sounded, and by sounding and resounding the water refined my soul more and more to the point where it could not hear or say, even by being what it doubtless was or said.

Then I noticed, out of the corner of my eye, that the long shadow of a man stood leaning on the dull whiteness, all alone and silent, all absorbed in listening, made into the sharp shadow of a man, another shadow like mine, at the railing of the staircase. It seemed to me that he moved casually and carefully nearer. Finally he spoke in a tone of voice which did not prevent me from listening to the water.

He said, "Listening to the water, eh?"

"Yes, sir," I answered, getting dreamily to my feet. "And you, too, seem to enjoy hearing it."

Between the two of us, I on a stony landing of the staircase, he on the other side at the railing where the water continued to come down, looking at us, an instant of each second, then fleeing, stopping perhaps a second to look up, talking down below, singing, smiling, sighing, losing itself, emerging, with hypnotizing presence and absence, with who knows what truth and what lies.

"I don't have to enjoy it, sir," he said, "when I've been hearing it for thirty years."

"Thirty years," I said to him from I don't know what date of my own and without quite realizing how many years I was mentioning.

"Just imagine the things *she* has told me." And he added, "The things I have heard."

And he slid down into the night and was lost in the darkness and the water.

Verso y prosa para niños/1936

NIGHT VISIT TO "THE HILL"

This Peak of the Wind, that today is called Hill of the Poplars—
they hold back the wind in their flourishing oasis and humanely
shelter us from it—how near it carries us to the zenith! On its
plateau in this night of April first, the lights from above and be-
low are here wholly intermingled, those hanging, the great
white dazzling stars, and the green gaslights, and the mallow-
pink balloons of electric lights, and the enormous, yellow moon;
it is as if they all emerged together from the level plain nearby,
in plebian and aristocratic confusion, from the suburbs of sky
and earth.

Solitude, silence among all the angles, planes and corners of
the promontory. And how welcome everything is—in its variety,
in its movement, in its organization—on this night climb of
mine after so many days! What a presentiment of new green in
the same dark blue, a profuse awareness, sensual and healthy, of
images painted and sung, dreams yearning through lonely
snow, lonely sunlight, and the loneliest flying hurricane! And
now, above the half-glimpsed little canal, how closely does the
song of frequent birds and the croaking of the friendly frog cor-
respond among cool, sweet garlands, among the labyrinth of
treetrunks, leaves and flowers. Rising suddenly after dying down
among the straight poplars with round silver leaves, how sim-
ilar the wind of today is to the wind of another time blowing
through unrestrained fancy!

I capture the cleanest of air with deep-drawn, contented breath.
What a sense of well-being indeed returns suddenly to body and
soul in this fresh, cool height! How intensely one always feels
here, at this level of lofty atmosphere, in spite of restricting
cares, the root of the attainable elite of the second Goethe which
we sow with the trees on a restless January midday. How pro-
foundly we always discover here and in every bit of this spot, the
modest, the sound, the uncontaminable, the chosen! A joyful

dance of all the celestial and terrestrial lights in joyful eyes! I suddenly start trotting upwards then downstairs straight toward the Guadarrama, vaguely amaranth as it falls upon us! From everywhere I run out smiling, happy, from my forgetfulness, in a multiple, open rose, to embrace myself!

Verso y prosa para niños/1936

THE BLIND MEN OF MADRID

They are coming from the concert, hurrying, laughing, joking, stimulated by the cold night, beneath the autumn leaves which the electric street lamps magically illuminate with sharp gold, beneath the liquid green stars (higher up)—black, shut in, black, black . . .

"How divine Mendelssohn is, isn't he? I don't care what you say! Now that's music!"

And the one who says this whistles in romantic extravagance, as if wholly penetrated by a celestial elixir, his big, white, round face full of the great shadow.

"Then what about Schubert?" (sings another voice, turning to the one before, pressing close to his lapels so that the two faces look up at the sky together), "Ah Schubert, my own Schubert!"

And his eyes roll up to the sky.

They all run silently now, drunk with an antiquated sentimentalism of waltzes and barcaroles, with their pure music; they are a tame herd of sheep not allowed to go free, this is the elegance, the delicacy (here the vulgar word makes one weep) of their poor souls, like those of sequestered women.

Suddenly in their impetuous and drunken career the ones in front realize that they are not followed by other familiar footsteps.

"Paco . . ."

"Paco . . ."

"Paco . . ."

And they begin to look here and there, still raising their eyes . . . Paco doesn't answer. Cold, dark silence.

Then they all huddle together in a melancholy way and stand still, their heads hanging, their blind eyes now on the ground, afraid of getting lost, like lambs, black, black, black.

Verso y prosa para niños / 1936

CITY OF THE SKY

In a night gleaming
With primal purity,
The City of the Sky high above,
Over a background of light from the coming hour,
The outline of the lovely earth arises.

(In a blue valley, all is full of
Precise, transparent atmosphere,
Which in gleaming quietude
Defines consummate beauty.

142

Elm trees grouped
At the fountain of lifegiving water
Shape a paradise entrusted to us,
An overall dark green murmuring
Around immortal emptiness.)

La estación total / 1923-1936

RETURNING FLOWER

The flower returns the same
To mark off the blue instant for us,
To offer a delicious brotherhood to our body,
And, immensely perfumed, to tell us
That brevity is enough.

Brevity in the golden sun, in the golden air,
In the golden earth, in the aureate sea;
Brevity against the sky and the gods,
Brevity in the midst of a dark no,
Brevity in sufficient action,
Balance between harmony and light.

And the flower sways with the richest
Perfume of flesh,
Perfume which enters the being and reaches to the end
Of endlessness and is lost there,
Making us into garden.
The living flower sways, without, within,

143

Its weight in exact ratio to its pleasure.
And the bird loves it and fills it with ecstasy,
And woman, curving, loves it,
And man loves it and kisses it.

To flower, to live, an instant
Of spark in the midst of things, at a standstill,
Opened in tempting form,
Instant without past,
In which the four points of the compass
Attract equally, sweet and profound,
Instant of love open
Like a flower!
Love and flower in perfection of form,
In mutual frenetic affirmation of forgetfulness,
In mad compensation,
Perfume, taste, and perfume,
Color, perfume and touch, perfume, love, perfume.

The red wind seduces it
And carries it off, delicious rape,
In a living fall which is a dying
Of sweetness, tenderness, freshness;
A falling of a flower in complete beauty,
Flying, passing, dying of a flower and of love
In the supreme day of beauty,
Leaving no sorrow in the world at its ardent departure,
Soothing the earth, sun, and shadow,
Losing itself in the eyes of the light!

La estación total / 1923-1936

FLOWERS BENEATH THE LIGHTNING

The flowers join hands
And fly off like birds.
They do not go.
(But they fly like birds.)

They pull, they swoop downward
Beneath the storm cloud with lightning.
They do not go.
(Beneath the storm cloud with lightning.)

They cry out with anguish, with white,
With yellow, and with tears.
They do not go.
(With yellow and with tears.)

Each thunderbolt with its dart
Wrings a cry from them in the lightning.
They do not go.
(Wrings a cry from them in the lightning.)

Their perfume is bitten and so intense
That the damp perfume is bleeding.
They do not go.
(The damp perfume is bleeding.)

They fly, as the birds flee,
Lest they dry up with fear.
They do not go.
(Lest they dry up with fear.)

The flowers join hands
And cry out like birds.

They do not go.
(But they cry out like birds.)

La estación total/1923-1936

I SHALL BE REBORN

I shall be reborn a stone,
And I shall still love you, woman.

I shall be reborn wind,
And I shall still love you, woman.

I shall be reborn wave,
And I shall still love you, woman.

I shall be reborn fire,
And I shall still love you, woman.

I shall be reborn man,
And I shall still love you, woman.

La estación total/1923-1936

THE COMING STAR

The star is in the orange tree.
Let us see who can capture it!

Come quickly with pearls,
Fetch nets made of silk!

What an odor of springtime
From its flask of eternal life!

The star is in all eyes.
Let us see who can capture it!

In the air, in the grass,
Take care, do not lose it!

The star is in love!
Let us see who can capture it!

La estación total / 1923-1936

WITH THE ROSES

No, this sweet afternoon
I can not stay indoors;
This free afternoon
I must go out in the open air.

Into the laughing air,
Spreading through the trees
Thousands of loves,
Profound and waving.

The roses await me,
Bathing their flesh.
No boundaries contain me;
I will not stay indoors.

La estación total/1923-1936

FORTUNATE CREATURE

You go singing, laughing through the water,
You go whistling through the air, laughing,
On blue and gold, silver and green rounds,
Happy to pass and repass
Among the first red budding of April,
Clear shape, with instants
Of light, life, color,
Similar to ours, flaming shores.

How joyful you are, being,
Filled with such eternal and universal joy!
You gaily break the waves of air,
You sway in contrast to the rippling of water!
Do you never need to eat or sleep?
Is all of springtime your territory?
Is all the green, all the blue,

All that flowers yours?
There is no fear in your glory;
Your destiny is to return, return, return
On your rounds of silver and green, of blue and gold,
For an eternity of eternities!

You give us your hand in a moment
Of affinity attained, of sudden love,
Of radiant concession,
And, at your warm contact,
In a mad vibration of body and soul,
We take fire in harmony,
Being new, we forget the feeling of sameness,
We shine, an instant, joyful with gold.
It seems we, too, shall become
Perennial like you,
That we shall fly from mountain to mountain,
That we shall leap from sky to sea,
That we shall return, return, return
For an eternity of eternities!
And we go singing, laughing through the air,
Through the water we laugh and whistle!

But you do not have to forget,
You are a casual, continual presence,
You are the fortunate creature,
The magical, single being, the sleepless being,
Adored for warmth and grace,
Free, intoxicating thief,
Who, on blue and gold, silver and green rounds,
Go laughing, whistling through the air,
Singing through the water, laughing!

La estación total/1923-1936

5

1940/Portraits of writers and artists

GUSTAVO ADOLFO BÉCQUER

Gustavo Adolfo Bécquer (1836-1870) was the most important roman-
tic poet of Spain. His work leads toward symbolism and is therefore
the beginning of all contemporary Spanish poetry. ED.

Bécquer stretches out a hand, throws himself into the encircling
seawind, and with it flies out of his great honeysuckle vine, his
momentary refuge from the sudden, thundering May downpour,
a welcome moment of gentle, fragrant shadow in his despair.
Trembling, cyanotic, coughing, at the same time clutching his
tall hat against the strong gust, with a hard struggle he wraps up
the imaginary harp in the short cape which hardly covers him in
this moment of cold green spring, full of whirlwind, dust, and

drops. Did he abduct it that morning in an obscure corner of the salon, its naked strings, full of sleeping wings like an almond tree in flower? Where is he taking it to open its notes? What a confusion: honeysuckle, oppression, spring, woman, gooseflesh, ideal, harp! Harp or woman, strings or arm, dream, all of intangible love:

(*Sealing his betrayal with a kiss.*)

He has an echo nailed in place in the center of his soul and he goes on suffering from it, as if from a magnified orange thorn, an unbearable angina pectoris which does not quite kill the first time. To endure so much enflamed agony and to see if he can drive it into the sea through the river of his blood, his heart, a muffled drum, drums louder still with its second aortic murmur, beating through his entire sense of hearing, from heel to temple, under a choking cloud, the sharp, dull assonance reinforced by a second poetic murmur, weighted with the dark, hypertrophied heart. Languid anxiety in definite reaction to the white, mallow-pink, and golden flights of fancy! And by this assonance of the heart, he transforms, makes his, and reaches the eternal since it is life, beat, the Spanish verse of his day:

(*Today the sun reaches the depths of my soul.*)

All around Bécquer, like the yellow and silver sum of the ideal flower, among birds all united to crown it, the ardent beak chirping at it, Rhyme flies, in so many cases before and after, a vulgar thing: unique and authentic in him as it is only his hard, grey assonance. Sound, Rhyme, indeed for many years they will not be used in Spain without a return to Bécquer. Sound, Rhyme, Rhyme, Sound. Rhyme, the Rhyme of the black and white breast preserved on the escutcheon of the portico, on the stone of the tomb, on the wall of the convent, on the closed balcony with the western sky of Seville, green and pink with water and sun, on its pane of glass. The Sound of the heart, the swallow-winged Rhyme. (Better romanticism, recondite, precise, hemmed in by the inevitable environment of the epoch.) The short Rhyme, Bécquer, the deep Sound.

Españoles de tres mundos/1940

ROSALÍA DE CASTRO

Rosalía de Castro (1837-1885) was a Galician poet who also wrote in Spanish. She was a writer of great originality. Her use of symbolism makes her, along with Bécquer, a forerunner of contemporary Spanish poetry. ED.

It rains in all of Galicia. Ground and sky are blended, the four-cavitied heart by its inner texture, by the rain. All of Galicia is encompassed by a great, muffled heart. The villages, uniform black churches, blacker, blackest with a primordial black brought out by the rain, reek of the damp human stable. Rosalía de Castro as she stands in mourning at the door of her house, is thinking of her field (house a bucket of maize, grapes, half granary), water flowing nearby. She sees it rain on the soft greenness, on the liquid earth, on the muddy water; she sees the faithful cow pass through water and more water, the colorless albino adolescent, the slovenly passer-by who greets her, the wooly pilgrim, the dirty priest, the sickly freckled girl, the little groaning cart. The bells of Bastabales toll softly, drowned in watery air:

(*Bells of Bastabeles,*
When I hear you ringing
I die with nostalgia.)

Poverty and solitude. Anxiety, grief, asphyxia from so much surrounding solitude and poverty. A large mouth, an ugly sympathy; they weep, despair, sob. Rosalía de Castro, tragic Galician lyricist, despaired, wept, and sobbed continually, her dress and her pain black, her body neglected, golden with soul in her own pool. Beautiful disconsolate, walled-in soul, isolated, buried in life! She is surrounded by human herds which are the same as inhuman herds: the same defeated heaviness, the identical inescapable odor, the same submissive, resigned sensuality. And Rosalía does not take care of herself, she cannot take care of herself. She goes mad from her inner rhythm, a fusion of weeping, rain, and churchbell heart. All of Galicia is a damp madhouse in which she is incarcerated. Galicia, a prison of windows, a sentence of water, mist, and tears, through which Rosalía sees only the warm depths of her soul.

Mist in Galicia. A floating mist, encircling cotton, a salty, whipped cream, a surrounding paraffin over the estuaries; that besieges the walls, that spreads over the beaches, that turns everything dim within it, whitish, indistinct. The ships enter blindly, they do not enter. The few people are lost in the melancholy, opaque whole. Far off, nearby, in her house, in her field, on the deserted shore, the distances in her native country are short, Rosalía de Castro takes long slow walks, short, impatient ones, around the four black rocks, the four wet walls. She is surrounded, nearby, far off, in each lonely house, lonely rock, twin tombs, full or empty, in an eternal evening of a Galician All Souls Day, by other poor Rosalías, older or younger, "Widows of the living and dead whom no one shall console."

Españoles de tres mundos / 1940

JOSÉ MARTÍ

José Martí (1853-1895) was a Cuban poet. America has few writers so universal as Martí, the Cuban patriot and liberator. He is one of the initiators of the symbolist movement in Spanish literature in which it was given the name of modernismo. ED.

Until Cuba, I had never really come to grips with José Martí. The country, the background. A man without a background of his own or in us but with one within himself, is not a real person. I always seek the background of men and things. The background reveals the true being and state of being of the man or thing. If I do not possess the background, I make the man transparent, the thing transparent.

And through this Cuba, green, blue and grey with sun, water, or hurricane, palm tree in spreading solitude or shrunken oasis, clear sand, scrawny ground pine (or little pines), plain, wind, thickets, valley, hill, breeze, bay, or mountain, so full of the progressive Martí, through all this I have reached the Martí of his own books and of the books about him. Miguel de Unamuno and Rubén Darío have done much for Martí so that Spain might know Martí better (their Martí, since the Martí in conflict with a bad Spain, lacking conscience, was the brother of those Spaniards in conflict with that Spain opposed to Martí). Darío owed him much, Unamuno considerable; and Spain and Spanish America to a large extent owed the poetic participation of the United States to him. Martí, with his journeys into exile (New York was to the exiled Cubans what Paris was to the Spaniards) brought the United States into closer contact with Hispano-America and Spain more than any other writer of the Spanish tongue, in the liveliest and most positive way. I believe Whitman, more American than Poe, came to all of us Spaniards through Martí. Martí's essay on Whitman which I am sure inspired Darío's sonnet to "The Good Old Man" in *Azul,* was the first introduction I had to the dynamic and delicate poet of *Autumn Brooks.* (If Darío had passed through New York, Martí had lived there). Aside from living in himself, in himself alone and looking at his Cuba, Martí lives (in prose and in verse) in Darío who nobly admitted his heritage from the very beginning. What he gave him amazes me today, now that I have read both thoroughly. What a fine gift and acceptance!

From the time when, almost a child, I read some verses of Martí's, I don't know where:

I dream of cloisters of marble
When in divine silence,
Standing upright, heroes repose:
And at night, in the light of the soul,
I speak to them, in the nighttime!

I "thought" of him. He did not leave me. I saw him then as someone rare and different, not indeed from us Spaniards, but from the Cubans, the Hispano-Americans in general. I saw him more upright, more steely, more direct, finer, more secret, more national, and more universal. A very different person from his contemporary, Julián del Casal (so Cuban in another way in that disoriented moment of half-understood *modernismo,* the false one) whose artificial work nevertheless brought Darío to us in Spain, and then Salvador Rueda, and Francisco Villaespesa afterward. Casal was never to my taste. If Darío was very French in the decadent sense like Casal, the profound and elemental Indian and Spanish accent of his best poetry, so rich and graceful, fascinated me. I have felt and expressed, perhaps, an inner preciosity, possibly an exquisite and sometimes difficult vision of a psychological process, "the landscape of the heart," or a metaphysical "landscape of the brain," but the exotic princesses, the Greek and Roman medallions, the "capricious" Japanese effects and the hidalgos of the "golden age" never conquered me. For me *modernismo* was a different sort of novelty, it was an inner liberty. No, Martí was something else and Martí was, by virtue of this "something else" very close to me. And how could anyone doubt that Martí was as modern as the other Spanish American modernists?

I had read little of Martí then, enough, however, to understand him both in the spirit and the letter. His books, like the majority of Spanish American books not printed in Paris, were rarely seen in Spain. His prose, so Spanish, perhaps too Spanish, with its excess of classical trimming, I scarcely knew. That is, I was acquainted with it and liked it without knowing it because it was in the "Cronica" of Darío. Darío's *Castelar,* for instance, could have been written by Martí. It was only that Martí never felt attracted, as Darío did, to that Spanish gaudiness which dazzled the latter, be it as it may, without thinking about it, like a wide-eyed, provincial child. Darío remained in many cases outside the "character," king, bishop, general or scholar, dazzled by the ritual. Martí never expressed enthusiasm over outward display, not even over women who meant so much to Martí (and to Darío but in a different way). Martí's only archaism was in the case of words and only those which stood for an idea or an appropriate sentiment. (This parallel between Martí and Darío I would not have felt without coming to Cuba.) And I have no intention, be sure, even in justice to Martí, of in any way minimizing the great Darío in the slightest since I admired and loved him for other qualities, and even for the same ones, and especially because he admired and loved and admitted that he owed so much to Martí, (I can testify to his spoken word). The difference, aside from what is inherent in the essence of two existences, was in the most profound depths of their two experiences, for Martí carried a Spanish wound within him which Darío had not received so directly.

This José Martí, this "Captain Spider," who spun his thread of noble love and hate among roses, words, and white kisses as he waited for destiny, fell in his landscape, which I have now seen, a victim of passion, envy, and perhaps indifference, as he was fated to, no doubt, like a knight-errant in love, of all times and all countries, past, present, and future. Cuban Don Quixote, encompassing the spiritually eternal and the Spanish ideal. Cubans, you should write the *Ballad* or the *Romancero of José Martí,* more than anyone else hero of life and death, who "exquisitely" defended his country, his wife, and his people by sacri-

ficing his lofty poet's life. The bullet that killed him was for him,
who doubts it, and for "that reason." It came, like all unjust bul-
lets, from many regions, and from many debased centuries, and
few Spaniards and few Cubans did not have a part in it, without
wanting to, an unconscious atom which entered into him. I, my-
self, do not feel that this atom was never in me, though it did
not belong to me, the atom which entered into him. I always
felt for him and through what he felt, what is felt in the light,
under the tree, near water, and with the flowers which are re-
spected and understood. I am of the ecstatic sort, one who be-
lieves the good (and Bruno Walter says this in another way,
Bruno Walter, the poet of music, pure and serene, exiled and
free, brother of Martí and, begging pardon for my egotism,
mine, too), who believes the good is "apparently" destroyed by
others but they do not destroy it "completely," as evil destroys
itself.

Españoles de tres mundos/1940

RUBÉN DARÍO

*Rubén Darío (1867-1916) was the greatest poet of the Spanish mod-
ernist school and one of the most important figures in contemporary
Spanish writing. Though born in Nicaragua, his influence extended
over all of the Spanish speaking world.* ED.

Five, seven, thirteen, seventeen times, my Rubén Darío. So much
Rubén Darío in me, always so alive, so consistent and distinct, al-
ways so new! None of my successive silhouettes (*My Rubén
Darío, For and against Rubén Darío, Rubén Darío, Spaniard,*
etc.) is the one that follows. And indeed the silhouette made
possible by his death filled me with sorrow as I set about writing
it just as when, sailing from Spain to New York in 1916, dur-
ing a most bitter February on an afternoon off Newfoundland,
blinded by a white cyclone, the radio saddened me with the

tragic news on one stage of the route that he, while still living a little in himself, had previously taken. (It was still possible here and there in New York to come upon the last traces of his hand, especially on the table of the Hispanic Society where he had left his last photograph with his signature still firm and rounded.)

Today now that I am closer to his León of Nicaragua and his body is no more, the caprice of an incessant wave of images raises a Rubén Darío of the sea in my imagination, an image which perhaps emerges from the photograph given me in Madrid years ago by the good and faithful Alfonso Reyes, always Rubén Darío's best friend, in contrast to those immense, rainy horizons of the coastal plains of Florida which extend down to the southwest, to Nicaragua. A Rubén Darío in the summer whites of a ship's captain.

. . . where a warm and golden afternoon . . .

Rubén Darío was always dizzy from the waves, from Venus, from the tonic salt. And so he never knew what to do with his frock coat, his gloves, his tall hat, and even less with his diplomatic disguise. This was not his proper costume either as a plenipotentiary favorite of his oriental queen or as an admiral of his god Neptune. A greater nakedness he kept hanging on the clothesrack of his lodging house. This was why he was sometimes found lying in the gutter; he got tangled up in his uniform. His round fat bulk, above little feet, like a shark standing upright on its tail, could not, I maintain, manage a waistcoat. At times I think of him as a faunlike dolphin-sultan of the coral reefs, among the mermaids of his aquatic harem. No, no, gentlemen, his perpetual rhythmic reeling was not so much the tipsiness of Noah as the heaving and tossing of the ocean. When he pulled out his anachronistic watch, I understood from the way he tapped it and the lost way he looked to the four winds, crossways of the salty unattainable, that what oriented him was a compass.

. . . as if it were a rude sound . . .

His true fatherland was the island of the Argonauts, of Cytherea, of Columbus. His favorite word, "archipelago." When he said it in his throat he seemed to be swallowing it down the gullet of a giant love-smitten sailor, as if it were a dozen oysters. Except as an oriental paradise for the divine and human species descended from Venus, for him continental lands had no other reason for existence. Always Venus, watching over him from his youth, island woman of green space:

. . . Venus, from the abyss was looking at me with sad glances.

In his certain glorification, Rubén Darío must have been destined by his pagan divinities (among whom Christ peeped out, a gentle visit which pleased him greatly) for an emerald isle. Green transparent island, oval in the west of the cerulean sea, great primordial and ultimate jewel, perennial apotheosis of hope fulfilled. For he saw eternity, too, like an island, symphonic finale of the everyday west, and the immortal awaited him as it awaits the nostalgic navigator. I have dreamed of him often, pirate captain of the entire marine treasury, goddesses, clouds, corals, constellations, mermaids, suns, pearls, winds. Treasurer of his own purpose, now free of that "exile" of the sea-journalist which was his melancholy, buskins of glory with no other utility than their Parnassian glory, shall be the adornment of his dwelling, floating between two kinds of space, air and water. The blue, the twin blue. Rubén Darío, more than any other, minister of the captains of the wind,

that turns the blue silk of the firmament to blood
with the red banner of the monarchs of the sea.

FRANCISCO GINER

Francisco Giner (1839-1915) was a great liberal educator active in Spain at the end of the nineteenth century. He influenced much of contemporary Spanish thought and founded the "Free Education Institution" in Madrid, in 1876. ED.

He came and went like a fire in the wind. And he rose up, a whistling viper of light, and he spread and burst into flame, a sparkling vine of coals, and he charged forward, a little flaming lion, and channeled himself in a trickle of pure gold; and he appeared here and there without visible unity, everywhere, thin, airy, intangible, with the unbounded elasticity of a diabolic flame. (What were the names, then, which were given, alive and dead, to this intense conflagration, those which so thoroughly misinterpreted him? What of "Little St. Francis," "Little Don Francis," "Don Paco," "Assisi," "Little Saint," "Paco"? No, no, he was nothing like that! To name him with something more than the name by which he called himself, Francisco Giner, or, as his most intimate friends called him, "Don Francisco," it would be better to say he was something like a spiritualized inferno.)

Good, doubtless, better than kind, extremely good, but from enjoyment, from true inebriation, from the impulse of the lover, from sorrow, from complete remorse. Yes, a joyful flame, condemned to earth, full of lively and thoughtful feeling, the surprised, anxious, prepared spectre, with sublimated passion, his material dry because it always longed for everything, but his soul fresh and abundant, a fountain of unquenchable blood in a summer field. And his innumerable tongues licked everything (rose, sore, star) in a constant loving renascence. He was all things, all things were in him: child in the child, woman in the woman, man as everyman, the youth, the sick man, the clever, the worst, the healthy, the old, the innocent, and tree in the landscape, bird, and flower, and, more than anything, light, gracious light, light.

The blending light which shot from the sword of his burning being crossed the whole sky from north to south, from east to west, in perennial incandescence, adding lustre to the day, reaching the end of each of his endless crossroads and penetrating into all the secrets of his moment. He cut, he kissed, he scorched, he died, he laughed, resurrected in every person and thing. One night, as in the oriental legend, the light which had this time gone very far (to do what?) did not have time to return to his sword at the right moment and sword and light were left alone, the former (what a little blue ember!) in its scabbard of earth, the light (sad and as if lost with its mastering liberty) wandering far and wide, no boundaries to its infinite, swaying wheatfield.

Españoles de tres mundos / 1940

JOSÉ ASUNCIÓN SILVA

José Asunción Silva (1865-1896) was a Colombian poet, a forerunner of the modernist school. He combined in his work romantic symbolism with the realism of the end of the nineteenth century. ED.

I like to imagine José Asunción Silva naked with his second and unique *Nocturne* in his hand. We need no other poem of his, no other portrait, no other biography, and the rest of his decadent life and confused writings I would burn: sateen interiors, foolish salons, Paris bindings, casino boasting, false polish, all that provincial, ridiculous, and empty dandyism which poor José Asunción put on, as did poor Julián de Casal, over his true spirit to astonish or mortify the more or less sensitive or tolerant Colombians of his day in an indifferent and blameless Bogotá.

Dandyism is always bad, above all an external dandyism, to the extent that it represents useless theatricality outside of time and space, extravagance in daily life. Authentic and realizable dandyism, however, may be understood and not resisted, that is when the dandy can be one wholly, when he is not a *cursi* [vulgarian]. I have heard in my own Andalusia that among the Moors, the Cursis were secondary chiefs who did not inherit a name or property, the "I want but can't" of the conforming aristocracy. Dandyism of the "I want but can't," a village imitation, seems nauseating to me. It is endurable, perhaps, in early thoughtless youth, since youth is accustomed to live externally, but not in adulthood. There are many classes of dandyism, many types; the more or less on the order of Petronius, the more or less Brummel, either before or since his well-known conception, grotesque or subtle dandyism, effete or violent, dandyism of Baudelaire, Wilde, D'Annunzio, Remy de Gourmont, Cocteau, Gómez de la Serna, Dali, etc. To disguise one's being in the protobeing X, I maintain, is aping, *cursiism* of a secondary sort. There is nothing more *cursi* than to imagine oneself a Mozart, a Goya, a Chateaubriand, a Goethe, to become comic oneself. The natural, the sincere is never *cursi,* nor is juvenile "sentiment" let it be as ingenuous, innocent, or simple as you wish. It is the copy that is *cursi*. Bécquer was not *cursi* because he was not a snobbish dandy; Silva was because of his frivolous parody of Paris, even to killing himself in the presence of other people. This portion of reflected dandyism is not, however, sentimentalism, sentimentalism is affection, generosity, felt through and for others: a dead child, the distant mother, an unfortunate sister, or for one's own suffering, solitude, sickness, etc., self-indulgence, yes, but not *cursiism*. It is the charity of St. Peter, noble negation. For this reason the marvellous nocturne of José Asunción Silva is not *cursi,* nor ever could be.

This nocturne, the germ of so much in so many, is without doubt the poem most representative of the last of romanticism and the beginning of *modernismo* which has been written in Spanish America. It fuses two tendencies or phases of idealism at

the exact moment which catches best, the most essential naked-
ness of each, and discards the excesses of each. It is naked poetry,
naked poet, naked woman, and for this reason it does not pass
away any more than do the naked picadores among the naked
bulls and horses of Picasso. It is poetry, written yet almost not
written, written in the air with the finger.

It has the quality of a nocturne, a prelude, an étude by an
eternal Chopin, which is called feminine because it is saturated
with woman and moonlight. Like a natural jewel of Chopin, a
naked torrent of Debussy, this river of melody of the Colombian,
who was marked by fate, (this spoken music, summation of love,
dream, spirit, magic, sensuality, human and divine melancholy)
I cherish in myself, in my body and soul, forever, and it forever
returns to intoxicate me and keep me vigilant.

Españoles de tres mundos/1940

ENRIQUE GRANADOS

*Enrique Granados (1868-1916) was a contemporary Spanish com-
poser famous for an opera,* Goyescas, *which was produced in New
York. Juan Ramón Jiménez here refers to Granados' trip to New
York and subsequent death when the steamship,* Sussex, *in which he
was returning to Spain, was sunk in 1916.* ED.

He entered in a double-breasted overcoat, a Scotch plaid muf-
fler up to his eyes, a little shawl in his hand, his popping eyes,
very convex like those of Socrates, looking half spherical as gen-
tle and kindly words came with good-natured laughter, through
his Asiatic moustache, with a Catalonian accent. Forgetting his
surroundings for a moment, in a corner he spoke to me of my
little *Platero* which he liked, he said, because it was sensitive and
ironical. Periquet then brought the songs that had to be trans-
lated very rapidly for the opening of *Goyescas.*

It was in New York, in 1916. Snow and soot, tubular

streets, blasts from an immense, all-encompassing chimney in whose bottom, completely cellar, myriads of diminutive beings like insects seen under a microscope, we among them, would here and there contribute bright colors and dulled lights from all countries against a background of strange coincidences and dissonances. Windows, containing life and death like a painter's canvases, another museum of windows, all the canvases of all the painters in the world. And everywhere (streets, parks, rooms) models for all the canvases in the world, even the rarest, epochs and styles superimposed. And many of us, emerging from our canvases or talking to ourselves, as one talks in New York, flying or trying to get somewhere.

Enrique Granados was afraid, horrified, this could be seen in both body and soul—horrified by what? By everything, by the sea, by the abstractness of New York, by the hotel, the theater, by people. His round good humor was tolerant but with what evident and undisguisable anguish! I heard him play the piano one evening, timidly, distantly, refined, as if excusing himself and hiding himself under that carnal Ana Fitziu, rotund and trembling, then half accepting the applause, without believing he deserved it, looking in another direction toward Pablo Casals who looked like an ecclesiastic and toward La Argentina dressed in the salon in showy scarlet.

The hurly-burly of New York caught Enrique Granados and carried him about (what an omen!) as the sea does a wreck, entirely at will. The all-encompassing dirty wave left him here or there, up or down, troubled or laughing. A vertical cyclone once snatched my tall hat, carried it up to the fiftieth floor in a narrow street and then dropped it rapidly, finally, like a period into a garbage can. And a spark from the firebox of the Sixth Avenue Elevated fell upon Granados between the muffler and the moustache. Scorched. Running, flying, melody in air or water.

In water. He fled to the sea, his greatest anguish. "If a lion pursues you, fling yourself into the sea." He was always in his stateroom, they told me. He peeped out a moment on deck, muffled up so as to see less, took fright at the elements and fled below, running, as if from something monstrous. From what did he fly? And the *Sussex* was torpedoed. For fear of the sea, Enrique flung himself into the sea with Amparo, his wife. All the rest remained on deck, there was no danger. They were seen for a moment, the other passengers looking down from above on a Charon's raft. They disappeared in the wave (he flying in horror, she, faithful lover, follower, jealous of the wave, of that fatal Venus)—forever.

Españoles de tres mundos/1940

MIGUEL DE UNAMUNO

Miguel de Unamuno (1864-1936) was perhaps the most important figure of Spain in the first third of the twentieth century. He achieved an international reputation as a novelist, essayist, poet, and intellectual. ED.

Has Don Miguel stepped out of his mountain range? And he hurls himself straight down upon us from the height, sharply, steeply, the hardest way, with the trajectory of a plunging eagle or a dolphin in the billowy sea, with the assurance of a dynamic sleep walker in this sleep of life, sleeping I say, awakened from the false reality of his life . . .

But what is this? Make way, make way for him! No, we were not here. It is just that Unamuno's person, when he comes from the burning yellow tableland, reflects red, silver, and black, svelte as a pine tree, he comes smiling but not laughing, hands in the pockets of his jacket, struggling (with his broad chest thrown out, with his keen eye, sharp as if spectacled, with alert ears) against the cyclone, the lightning, and the thunder of midday, like David against the Philistines, like Samson and the lion cub . . . and there's no Lion! Down with Goliath!

Careful, don't wake up or we shall lose the image . . . don't push any harder . . . this way we shall never reach him or he us. Wait your turn! And Don Miguel, like a Lutheran St. Christopher, crosses the desert which I maintain is now sea with sand, with the Child Jesus, a little lead Catalonian, with the esthetic Mediterranean up to his rugged knee . . .

Once more everyone make way, he is blinding us with fire, a burning like the greater cold of ice, the cyclone of gold that brightens everything. And Unamuno, naked, classic, Christian polychrome statue with precise hair, in Puerta del Sol, Madrid, plays ball with the green books in the bookstores of Fe and St. Martin . . . a viscous suicide with a scale is nearby and a shivering grasshopper playwright, naked, too, in the summer sun, before a jury of smiling sculptors . . .

Silence, terrestrial and celestial calm, Let's see. What a cool perspiration! The siesta is over and a soft, clear-colored evening falls. What an event! If there is not a soul in the landscape, seen through the window! Only smooth sky and smooth earth. It must be that Don Miguel de Unamuno, during this August siesta, stretched out on his bed in his clothes, was dreaming, in Salamanca, of coming to Madrid this winter. And in his hard, dry dreams, which were reflected against our walls in echoes of stonings, he was trying an absolute curve, a low straight ball game, a close definitive boxing match, against the thin air of the southwest and the edges of illusory crystals.

Españoles de tres mundos/1940

JOSÉ ENRIQUE RODÓ

José Enrique Rodó (1872-1917) was an Uruguayan essayist and intellectual whose work had great influence during the period in which

*the modernist school triumphed. He held an ideal of classic serenity
in philosophical thought.* ED.

I have always seen Rodó motionless as a statue. His work is a
plaster cast of an illustrious man; it is designed to achieve this
result. His prose, being of a generic type, free in spirit but with
individual elements, holds up well in the blue air. The century
to which he gave stature in his America endures by virtue of its
limitations. His relationship to Greece, Rome, Spain, and France
lent Rodó a beautiful base of indestructible stone and he piled
his own blocks upon it in the shape of a columned temple, a new
promontory. For me, Rodó treads the lofty levels of the classics,
a pilgrim whose foot is fit for the immortal flagstones with their
perennial tender grass; he is a permanent guest of museums,
libraries, gardens of the better periods, open to a slow sun.
Through him, good American as he was, who wanted to make
his Uruguay into an eternal seat of learning, we see his Monte-
video as an Athens, a Florence, a Salamanca, a Paris. Since man
has three beautiful faces: that of love, that of prayer, that of poetry,
Rodó endeavored to unite these three in one.

A mysterious activity caught some of us young Spaniards
when, around 1900, Rodó was mentioned in our meetings in Ma-
drid. *Ariel,* in the only copy known to us, went from hand to
hand, filling us with amazement. How dreamlike was my wish
to possess then those three little thin books, neat and blue with
sharp red and black letters: *Ariel, Rubén Darío, He Who Is to
Come!* Afterwards, in 1902, I had a priceless letter from Rodó
apropos of my poor, sick, *Rhymes.* Then, for me alone, his longed-
for books. Later in 1908, his critical work, *Recondite Andalusia,*
in return for my fervid elegies. Finally *Protean Themes, Pros-
pero's Belvedere.* Afterward . . .

Altogether dark and ruddy, a confused and sanguine empha-
sis, thick, vigorous, American treetrunk, José Enrique Rodó
arose briskly from his armchair and stood upright. A good

friend of us both presented us. What an unlooked-for surprise was mine! How unaware I was on that radiant Madrid morning that Rodó was "awaiting me," without my knowing it, in the editorial office of *España* on Prado Street, then presided over by Ortega y Gasset and "Fígaro"! How unaware I was that that beauty, that tall, pure, enameled bluegreen Madrid of foliage and granite, surrounded with the solemn stateliness of a mausoleum, a man they needed so, who already bore his definitive transformation in his dynamic blood. How unaware I was that that corner of a museum, of a botanical garden, of an academy had already sent the message of concession to its peers in Florence; how unaware I was that a sea, an Atlantic land, fit for the pilgrim, all lay forever behind Rodó. And how can destiny be altered?

Yes how stupidly unaware I was that that brief encounter between us was an acquaintance with his quick presence and a final farewell; how unaware I was that this fine, strong, healthy traveller, this lofty and generous master, fulfilling his inexorable destiny, was going swiftly and directly through my Spain to meet death in the ideal Italy on his way to Greece.

Españoles de tres mundos/1940

MANUEL DE FALLA

Manuel de Falla (1876-1947) was a distinguished, internationally known Spanish composer who lived in Granada for many years. One of his most familiar compositions is his suite of dances, "The Three-Cornered Hat." ED.

He went off to Granada for silence and time, and Granada surfeited him with harmony and eternity. A passerby on the Antequerela Alta sometimes sees a thin, neat, black presence with white trimmings, a black piano key standing among simultaneous leafage of a high second garden, or reddened by the sun, brick dust of a harsh, ragged sunset chirping with martins, a Sunday group of people (sherry and biscuits) around the table in the lower garden: the romantic slenderness of Granada darkened with lace, the old woman always lovely in a cloak of a bygone fashion, a frivolous foreign ballerina, the child, Maceo, with a head like a cocoanut, some Spanish poet.

His profound vigor, unequaled afterward in the music of his time, Falla treasured, in weekly seclusion, flinging himself into the cumulous dark green waves of the steep avenues of the Alhambra, like round enticing arms leading off into the intensely delicate last amethysts, opals, and pinks of sunset over the Sierra Nevada (the truth of Théophile Gautier), or sometimes from the Church of San Nicolas facing the scarlet cubes of the square, massive architecture of its towers, lonely and quiet beneath the continual heavy branching of richly veined evening clouds, or standing in front of the everlastingness of some unfunereal cypress, silhouetted entirely against a gay moon rising from a perennial white villa.

At night the noises of Granada arise: cries of children, bells, bleatings like tiny stars (for we are among the large ones), a cornet, fragments of popular songs, quavering laments, and the incessant lights of the orchards come and go. Solitude is complete in Antequerela where that green balcony stands out, that green shutter, that green street lamp (in the gutter a dead rat). And the corner, secret with dramatic temptation, goes on taking on time and meaning while, hiding in the shadow of the moon, the musician's dream hovers, happy and smiling after having told its beads, haunted by a rhythmic ghost with tempting whispers of occult, coppery, far away, gypsy song.

Españoles de tres mundos/1940

ANTONIO MACHADO

Antonio Machado (1875-1939) was one of the great contemporary Spanish poets whose name, along with that of García Lorca, was mentioned by the Swedish Academy when it awarded the Nobel Prize to Juan Ramón Jiménez in 1956. ED.

I only see him approaching as he walks around the tower on the ancient, grassy, red footpath, walking carefully as if he did not wish to step on the little flowers of the leafy sky which must come tumbling down from his fancy. Now that he is near me, stumbling awkwardly over a stone, I feel that he grows huge, rising suddenly like a black shadow that steps in front of a lighted backdrop or like a thick tree, when we reach the moment, that we do not find again, in which his unusual height is seen for a moment in the air.

Like the ordained musician of feeling, Antonio Machado walks the "shores of the sea" outside the walls of his own earthly cities (Soria, Baeza, Madrid) heavily, both slowly and majestically, in a straight line, with a torn book in his hand, remote from his own monotonous wandering. (I saw, in his house at the western end of Fuencarral Street, a picture by his brother, José, in which the young Antonio, playing cards with his grandmother and lost in thought with the card suspended in his hand, is glancing with an absent, transparent smile toward the Triana jasmines of his ethereal mother's balcony). This smile among the merlons of his teeth is like the eternal hedge mustard, filtered with light on top of a rampart by our southern sea (El Puerto, Rota, Sanlucár), weathered and crumbling.

Anything suffices for his smile and to everything his smile is appropriate. He does not see his own big body and is accustomed to exist entirely for himself, in his own head, when actually he means so much to others for his thick presence is a static past and his beautiful absence is a vivid actuality. Like a solitary ox in my Fuentepina, he circles around a pump at the end of an orange orchard, around a point in time in which the water, which never ceases to flow through the spout of the dead hours, is never forgotten, nor that water which has not yet shimmered into stars (profound dark shadow extending below) in the elastic reflecting basic substance of everything.

When Antonio Machado goes away, I always think of him raising the playing card, thinking distractedly (eternal land sailor) of his brother, who voyages across the farthest Spanish seas, constant and confused hero of his *Of the Road,* that secret little book of alleys and walls of a sad, choked horizon.

Españoles de tres mundos/ 1940

TERESA DE LA PARRA

Teresa de la Parra (1891-1936) was a contemporary Venezuelan novelist. Although she wrote only two books, they continue to be read for their sensitivity, sincerity, and grace of style. ED.

I only saw Teresa de la Parra once. She arrived heavily furred, breathing a restrained warmth, her grey greenish blue eyes sparkling transparently with sweetness and refinement. She was, how does one say it, "delicate." Her voice, wrapped in silk, more or less spoke from death.

Then she went to the Sanatorium of Fuenfría, in Guadarrama. From there she sent us her book, *Memories of Mama Blanca,* and when I finished reading it, I sent her a book of mine with some sincere words. We often thought of going to see her and did not get around to it. But I believed that death, which spoke in her voice, was going to remain in those garrets of the being where we all have so much death, so many dead, and that the sounder islands of her body would resist indefinitely the siege of the worst poisons in the bloodstream. It was not so.

Little and ugly poison conquered greatness and beauty as so
often happens in life. And today I read (in *El sol*) the sadly con-
firmed news of her silent death.

Teresa de la Parra, a Venezuelan of Spanish origin (Valencian
and Basque) left us her true voice written in clear Spanish. Her
expression was poetic narrative which united the lyric and the
ironic in a delicate and gracious natural speech. She lightly burst
all fetters, being one of those enchanting forms of Spanish which
have lingered in certain American cities (as they have in pro-
vincial Spanish capitals) great paradises on the other side of the
sea, of whose colors, hours, and beings I have dreamed ever since
I was a child, perhaps more of them than of those paradises in
nearby Spain. It seemed to me that Teresa de la Parra came to
"her" Spain from "my" Spain. From a Spain remembered, loved,
and desired. I had certainly known her in dreams in some cor-
ner of the immense, Spanish paradise, and enjoyed hearing her
speak in her fluid tongue, my tongue of a relative time (during
that hour she actually passed beside us, too, so gentle, so agree-
able, so simple) as one enjoys hearing an old unforgettable
friend.

Lydia Cabrera told us that the morning before Teresa de la
Parra died, Lydia, who was looking after her, made a little
coffee. And she asked her if she would not like to try some.
Teresa de la Parra (I, remembering her voice, can imagine very
well her tone at the moment) answered, "I will eat a little earth."
Yes, we all have to eat this bit of earth before we die and we
shall never know, while alive, where it will be, where it will be
awaiting us, mixed with air, this bit of earth that we shall eat, an
aperitif to the great meal, the earth which, until we ourselves
are made earth, will never be absent from the corner of our
mouths.

Teresa de la Parra, white, fleeting passer-by, I do not know if
you have heard me say that we all must, like you, eat this bit of
earth which, for you, was Spanish. Now you remain among us

Spaniards. Here your moments were doubtless days, your days months, your months years. You have not lived "less." You had the power to extend what was brief, to make a look endure, and to make your voice stay with us, meaningful, lasting. Here you are not dead, your feminine presence still lives on from one afternoon. You stopped, drawn by the core of the earth of mother Spain who had heard you speaking slowly and kindly with her own voice, in her lofty air.

Españoles de tres mundos / 1940

6

1941/Ideas on society and poetry

ARISTOCRACY AND DEMOCRACY

If, to express disagreement with a better individual, and in sup-
posed defense of a supposed popular ideal, there is an outcry
against "aristocracy" (as frequently happens), two falsehoods are
being unconsciously and gratuitously entertained: one, conces-
sion of the concept "aristocracy" to the false, ostentatiously privi-
leged, and the other a more or less honest attack upon true aris-
tocracy, taking it for granted that it consists of a false manner.

And what is aristocracy and what is democracy, you false
aristocrats and cannibalistic democrats, enemies of the humble
aristocrat?

In these United States, which do not carry the heavy and at
the same time hollow burden of traditional aristocracy or the
ambiguous democracy of so much of the old world, where we

do not need to get rid of any prejudicial difficulties to reach the simple truth which is surrounded by these prejudices and in conflict with them, it is easy for me to clarify for myself what the two are, especially in the social sphere, and what they can not be in the sense in which they are understood by much of old Europe. Here the so-called "people" is in an ascending phase of well-being, it possesses a just and attainable culture, more evident and more firmly grounded than in the rest of the civilized world that I am acquainted with, even though the danger exists that this people in full career may become stagnant through the lack of ideals inherent in this very quotidian well-being, through becoming a "middle class," a bourgeoisie similar to that of the old world and also certainly farther from the people and from true aristocracy than anywhere else in the world.

Aristocracy, in my opinion, is a state of man in which are united in supreme union, a profound cultivation of the interior being and a conviction of the natural simplicity of living—idealism and economy. The most aristocratic man will then be he whose spirit needs least from the outside, without discounting what is necessary, and also does not long for the superfluous. And what is democracy? Yes, etymologically democracy signifies the rule of the people and, in order to rule, the people has to cultivate itself fundamentally in body and in spirit. But, when so cultivated, the people is already an indisputable aristocracy so that there is no democracy in the logical sense because there is no contrast between people. The people, moreover, could not govern as such a people ordinarily is, as a people in the state in which its exploiters keep it, in reality it is a half-stagnant bad bourgeoisie which wishes to rule without *demos* or *aristos*. And it is not just that the people should remain in the plebian phase, an amorphous rustic mass in which it is now in a good part of the world, thanks to its bloated defenders. I do not believe in a humanity massed together and more or less equalized by these or those advantages, but in a struggled-for community of completely individual men. I do not now think it necessary then to define democracy because, in my opinion, it is only a pathway, a better staircase to an attainable aristocracy, a progressive negation which dries out this mass (which bears a price tag as in an advertisement to buy or sell, a secret even from the one who advertises) in proportion as it approaches its superior state. In this sense democracy is a negative concept, a mistaken one, negligible, just as aristocracy, in the sense in which I wish for it, is an affirmative concept and a perennial one which well supports its shadow. In any case, if it must be defined, democracy should be what is not yet truly aristocratic and no more than that.

Concepts frequently come to life and go on living in this mistaken way and are founded on some lie, on great fabrications with unsound bases such as the concept of "classicism," for example. A work will be "classic" one day if it has retained life and quality enough to reach the concept and merit it. This is why, for example, the fifth century Greeks are classic. What happens, I maintain, is that the classics, those which have conquered time and space with their vital truth, are confounded with those which pretend to have done so without conquering anything. We say that a classicist is a classic or to increase the confusion, a neoclassic when he is a pseudoclassic. Thus the same thing happens in another way and in another sense with the concepts of democracy and aristocracy. No one is a democrat, as no one is aristocrat, just as no one is a classic by imitating a more or less antique historical tradition. If an exceptional man with all his defects as a man of his epoch (and the best of all men have them, fortunately) Leonardo da Vinci, to take the best example of a man both cultivated and tolerant who achieved fulfillment of his consciousness every day, if such a man was an aristocrat and a true democrat in his life and work (he who succeeds in being an aristocrat inevitably sustains the democrat converse) then the descendants or heirs of such a man will not be aristocratic or democratic by merely following him, or, in turn, their heirs or

followers; they will be aristocraticists and democraticists, Leon-
ardists in any case. No one will be a progressive aristocrat or
democrat except he who by faithfully carrying on his life and
work merits this appellation anew. And if this situation occurs
in the case of the exceptional man who merits every good name,
what about the negative man, hollow roots of a more or less
leafy genealogical tree?

The aristocrat, I insist, can not be truly so by descent, by be-
ing a link in some chain of generally accepted past social pre-
eminence, nor can the democrat be so through some confused,
progressive ambitions in regard to the future. As I understand
it, a complete reversal of the situation is needed to put aristocracy
and democracy in their proper places. Democracy is doubtless a
concept of the past because it is aspiration more or less clearly
stemming from the secular injustice in the world; aristocracy is
a concept of the future because it looks toward final justice in
the world. This certainly ought to convince us and to assure the
mistaken person, that we are not aristocrats by descent from
some famous human mixture with heads of bulls or serpents,
with heraldic devices more rhetorical than poetic, or above all
because some ambiguous unidentified ancestor ferociously kills
many Moors or because he aids some king with alleged gold;
and we are just as little democrats because we spring from
some hateful being, the slave of deprivation and disdain. We are
aristocrats because we rise or wish to rise to a state of being
which we all ought to be creating because we aspire to create
and are creating our superior selves, our finest descendants. We
participate truly and progressively in this rising up to the
greatest potential of the future and not in a falling back in every
sense to a retrogressive minimum, some bestial "hero" of the
two-handed sword or the ark. Etymologically, too, aristocracy
means no more than government of the best men, the most no-
ble, of the men proven to be virtuous. And democracy ought to
mean the same thing. Consequently, in this sense, the word de-

mocracy is superfluous, is as little use to us, and today more so than ever, because the people can be and often is the greatest and most noble class, the people can be the good. And if, as all the conventional aristocracies repeat, God was the beginning, we all come from God, and God must likewise be, assuming this, the termination of everyone's aspiration and the democratic sum, for is not God going to embody the people within himself? He would be the supreme and longed-for man.

2

The Spanish people (in this lecture I am now giving I refer particularly to Spain because it is the country I really know and through it all the old countries), the worthy peasantry, I say, not the proletariat, a different aggregate, is in Spain generally an authentic and primitive aristocracy. It is *demo* and *aristo,* that is, the best people and by its existence clearly demonstrates the wrong we do when we employ words, wordiness, to characterize it pro and contra. I, who have travelled much in Spain, have encountered among my people, and more often in the solitudes of the country, the best examples of a congenital and progressive aristocracy. I attribute this to the general tempering, to the individual culture which is produced by daily contact with a natural environment as sober and as exquisite at the same time as that of Spain. I point out this contact because I believe that in order to be aristocratic all men, all peoples, all countries have to live united with their natural environment, with nature in general, for in it indeed we encounter daily symbols and signs which we then have to interpret in terms of the complete social life. Nothing contributes a better tempering, a more exact sense of propriety, nothing absorbs and annuls the petty, like nature, or like it isolates us and raises us to greatness. And even when we seem to ourselves or to others smaller in nature than in the city (this external contrast is less in your New York which is a natural environment of buildings) we are nevertheless as large as the nature in which we live. Everyone knows this who has given himself fully to nature, everyone who has compared his situation as a man with nature. The urban man is an uprooted tree, he can put out leaves, flowers and grow fruit but what a nostalgia his leaf, flower, and fruit will always have for mother earth! The Spanish peasant is a pantheist and a mystic and therefore delicate, fine, generous, because he loves, for mysticism and pantheism are love and love is a good sign of aristocracy. He loves his elemental land, air, and fire and by this constant love, the stone, the blue, harmonizes with his life. To become a whole being in the sense of attaining social justice, he only needs to be situated in an economic form with a simplicity and dignity different from those which he every day enobles with his own life. Thus the Spanish people would be perfect in the situation in which this people of the United States is today, it would be completely on the road to the ideal through the intensity of its passion and its behavior. But how little do we understand, we Spaniards of an absurdly superior class, and how badly do we get along with this extraordinary people of ours! How little we, who are aided by the noble masses, do to aid them and to develop and establish their organic freedom!

A Spanish and Andalusian writer, Salvador Rueda, who tried to put all the color of both the urban and peasant people of Spain into verse, could have been great, popularly great, if he had cultivated himself profoundly as was proper to one born of the people, as he was, and not in the foreign artificiality for which he had so little feeling. When he went to a popular fiesta in Madrid, which pleased him as if he had been a child, he put on the worst kind of espadrilles, "to seem of the people," he told me. And when he went about in these sandals he did not want to come up to see me in my house because he believed that he would offend what he supposed were my aristocratic tastes. "What ideas this Salvador Rueda has!" I thought, "who thinks he will offend me with sandals and the people with boots!" I, even though I was a youngster and he a man of fifty, said to him, "As far as I am concerned, I like to have you come to my house in espadrilles if you believe you ought to wear them but not in ones you dirty especially for the occasion. Where you ought not to go with these dirty espadrilles is to popular fiestas." And it was true that he did not seem at all of the people on account of his espadrilles but rather because of his good-natured artisan's face which created an absurd contrast when Salvador Rueda put on yellow, squeaking calfskin boots in order to appear at a literary party given by Don Juan Valera, a jocose plebian novelist generally considered in Spain a great aristocrat of life and, alas, of the novel. No, poor and far away Salvador Rueda, with the spirit of the people not realized in you, now earth in your popular earth, neither shabby espadrilles to seem of the people nor yellow boots to please the showy academicians. There is no need to deceive the people or such aristocrats, there is no need to deceive yourself—ordinary shoes, comfortable, simple, and clean, shoes of the best style and as durable as possible, are what the aristocrat and the democrat need, what we all need.

The man who is conscious of his being and his existence displays his aristocracy by not disguising himself from the people, by never lacking respect for his people whom he must help properly in these or other matters. Man should appear everywhere as he is, as his culture and cultivation have made him, without concessions to his environment or to fashion when such concessions do not derive from his own convictions. To avoid seeking notoriety is a good sign and a good law, it is also a good sign and a good law to make use of whatever suits a person best, even at the risk of alienating others. Don Miguel de Unamuno, a great man and a great individualist in so many things but with a Basque-Castillian confusion of the *demo* and the *aristo* which was terrible and irremediable, from the time I first knew him always wore a black jacket buttoned up to

the neck without a tie and an insignificant little soft hat, the
smallest hat imaginable, which on him looked like a black comb
on an angry black rooster. We all formed a picture of him like
this, we saw him like this everywhere and at all times without
anyone paying much attention. One day near the end of his
life, when his personality and his work were already estab-
lished, during the third Spanish republic, in order to go to
the palace to see the president, he took off his jacket and hat
and put on a collar and a fashionable tie, something that he had
never done under the monarchy to visit the King, "my king"
he once called him in the Atheneum, to my amazement and to
the amazement of all present. How curiously vulgar and feature-
less Don Miguel appeared to me when I saw a photograph of
him leaving the palace among the reporters, thus disguised,
how insignificant and different from himself, from his usual self,
from the tried and true Don Miguel! No, Don Miguel de Una-
muno, poisoned and impoverished by various people and by
yourself, you did not have to deceive those false aristocrats by
deceiving the people. A simple, ordinary suit like everyone else's
or one justified by your personality, neither elegant nor elaborate,
is good everywhere, in a cabin or a palace, as long as there are
cabins or palaces. You don't need to take your necktie off or
put it on. You, who taught us so many things, you, who were
always so conscientious, and you who never laughed or wept
all your life but only sighed or smiled in such an aristocratic
way, how could you forget all this?

Shoes, jackets, ties, collars, it seems these are important to our
existence! And now we come to the Spanish beard. In Spain the
beard is another touchstone. In Spain there are many traditional
beards, and many individuals among my people as well as many
of the bourgeoisie and the aristocrats wear beards. And why not,
why should a rich man wear one and not a poor one, a doctor
and not a carpenter, a painter of clouds and not one of doors? A
Spanish writer, now in his fifties, whom I know very well, who,

even though he was born in a bourgeois family, spent much of his time from his childhood on among the people wore a beard as can be seen from the first portrait which Joaquin Sorolla painted of him in Madrid. When the terrible "uncivil" foreign war began in which barbarians of every species and from everywhere bled and destroyed our Spain, in certain areas government officials took beards for a sign of aristocracy, a false aristocracy, I mean, because generals and friars on the other side wore beards. The anarchists who had certainly always been painted as wearing beards, or as not shaving, looked upon beards with hostile eyes, eyes in faces wearing a week's stubble. I am now going to read a short and very amusing and colorful quotation from an honest war novel written by my friend Ernestina de Champourcin . . .

"To some ingenuous people anyone who expressed himself in a cultured fashion and with refined manners was inevitably a fascist. And consequently I could cite the case of a poet who with generous élan joined the side of the people from the first day, unconditionally offering his material and spiritual aid, who was a victim, like some others, of a lamentable confusion. Africa, his friend and admirer, had asked him to come to the children's shelter to amuse the children with his conversation, a delicious mixture of imagination and wit which always developed new and fascinating colors when he came in contact with children, for proximity to them always enchanted the poet. But not all who worked in the house appreciated this fragile gift. On this particular day the militiamen of the guard, who were changed continually and at random without reference to party or affiliation, being unacquainted with the personality of the visitor and no doubt alien to all cultural manifestations, fastened exclusively upon his refined appearance and the dark, carefully combed beard which framed a pale face full of profundity and amiable spirituality. 'With a beard like that he can't be anything but a fascist,' one of the militiamen announced. 'If he doesn't go soon, I'll shave him,' added another voice with far from tranquilizing gestures. Africa, herself, became a little worried over this absurd attitude and the poet, sadly folding his wings had to disappear, seeking a more propitious climate for the immateriality of his flight . . ."

And so, according to the novelist, this writer, aspiring all his life to aristocracy, did not wish to disguise himself from his people during the war, whether they were anarchists or not, by shaving his beard because it would have been an ignoble gesture both cowardly and unworthy of the militiamen whom he treated in every other way as equals, and because shaving his beard would also have been an offense to his peers or equals, doctors, ministers, engineers, artists. "And the curious thing," said the astonished writer, "is that Lenin had a beard and so did Marx and the militiamen put pictures of Lenin all around although it seems they did not see them." Afterward the war produced the usual intermingling and many militiamen, even to El Campesino himself, wore beards everywhere. Another writer, who told the one cited by the novelist that he should shave his beard to avoid danger, let his own grow again to pass as a militiaman, to deceive the militiamen and the people with an unkempt beard.

These quotes and examples and others I will read later, I have not brought up out of idleness or to amuse, but sadly and with good reason. We live by example and example is what makes me always think over and write down my lectures because I want them to be lectures in the real sense of the word. Around absurd intrigues of apparent pettiness like the above, almost all of Spanish life is centered, a life of small change, shrieks, and fussing, with or without beard, with a buttoned jacket or a fashionable tie, with shoes shining from polish or with dirty espadrilles. And also the life of the other old countries, I imagine. And the new ones—will, in time, this dross of the old ones overtake them, too?

3

Wherever true aristocracy exists, in Spain or anywhere else, it necessarily has a non-sectarian religious character, it being understood that the sectarian can not be aristocratic. The aristocrat attains through himself, and perhaps by means of examples freely chosen from others, to the qualities which we ascribe to a saint or god, a spiritual god. Francisco Giner, the most complete man I have known in Spain who, through his kindness, I was able to know well, who is being forgotten so quickly by our democracies (the conventional aristocracies never did esteem him) was a fulfilled aristocrat. Gandhi, for example, is today a fulfilled aristocrat. This religious character that I speak of is likewise present in the best sense in a democracy in full career, a democracy like that dreamed of as the norm of free men by Tolstoi who was another indubitable aristocrat, not by descent but by inspiration. If the aristocrat is religious, he needs to be so only in essence, least of all by being a member of some congregation based on rewards and punishments (denying this world to merit the next) but he can be an aristocrat even as a member of such an organization. He needs no rewards either in this or in the other world, no rewards that are not within the self, in his society, in his solitude. He is a free aristocrat, profoundly in love with this life in which he must find everything and he does not believe he has to transcend it anywhere else as was the notion of the Catalonian poet, Juan Maragall in his "Song of the Spirit." His unique reward is his good and beautiful life, a mountain, a hand, a star, his reward is his peaceful death. Peaceful death, another superior concept, superior in its beautiful and sufficient eternity.

Rainer Maria Rilke, the German poet, who considered himself a pantheist and a mystic even in the sense of the religious and angelic, was an adulator of false aristocrats, above all women, even though he was also an admirer of scientists and artists. Taxed with being a snob by a woman friend of his whom I, too, knew, he answered more or less that he loved princesses because their blood and their jewels were antiquity, tradition, and traditional culture as much as a castle rampart or a church wall. I still from this life ask Rilke, even though he is now buried near the rusty wall of a Swiss church, "Traditional culture of what sort, the truth or a lie, justice or indignity, benevolence or cunning?" The people is older and more cultivated in blood and song, impalpable jewel, closer to the rampart of the castle and the wall of the cemetery, more weathered by the elements, the primitive ones, water, fire, air; the people is richer in concepts. By his Muzot wall, does Rilke see now that the people gave its soul to the rampart and the tower, from outside of it all, or that they filled the rampart and tower with the most intense light and that his aristocrats lived inside them, in safety and enjoyment?

There is no more exquisite form of aristocracy than living out of doors. When a man can live tranquilly out of doors without fear of anyone or anything on earth, or in space, and not because he is a savage but because he is thoroughly civilized, he has arrived through himself at the ultimate, that is to say the primal, having rid himself of all that is useless and unserviceable. Yes, this return to the primal is the ultimate to which a man can attain while he is alive, it can make him complete, master of God and himself, absolute friend to others, a poet without needing to write, without an academy.

I have seldom heard a conventional aristocrat boast of descent from a scientist, an artist, or even a saint unless the saint has also been a king and in the latter case more on account of the king than the saint, "And he was a saint, too." I have seldom heard a conventional aristocrat boast of descending from a supposed or true inwardness but always from outward dominion or from material force (and earlier I alluded to this in reverse). This shows very clearly the selfish basis of these aristocracies.

Don't such aristocrats sometimes understand that well-being is not gained by such a preoccupation but through quite different ones? To return to my book of examples, in Spain it is common to hear the so-called aristocracy or the crudest bourgeoisie, which looks to the nobility for its sad ideal, speak of the people with patronizing admiration. "What fine fellows there are among the people, aren't there? They are worthy, sober, even honest. And you know bread and sardines are all they need to live on. And how they enjoy whatever they get! More than we do turkey and pork. Just look at those children, they eat nothing but bread and cabbage and what fat bellies they have (they shouldn't have them, poor things!). It's all for the best that they should stay like this. They need nothing more and they don't get sick very often. They never call a doctor. Their brass chair, their pine table, their pitcher—surely they are better off than we are!" This "It's all for the best that they stay like this," and "They are better off than we are," does it perhaps spring from two convictions? One is doubtless the miserable and egotistic desire that things should stay like this; the other perhaps an unconfessed, subconscious suspicion that in reality the people *"are* better than they" since this simplicity is the aristocratic simplicity which all ought to possess, which all must possess, which all shall someday possess, thanks to loving comprehension, fraternal loyalty, and true justice.

I remember a statement which a young marquesa, daughter of a countess (who was "very religious" according to her own story), made to me: "Mama always says her cook is better off than she is." I answered, "Then tell your mother that she should change with her cook or at least one day be the countess and the next day the cook." She replied, "What things you say! You take everything literally! And 'class,' how is that going to be changed?"

Class. These people to whom their confessors attribute unique religious culture, to whom their periodicals attribute their other kind of culture, divide society into people who belong to a "class" and those who belong to "no class." They have a book in which classes are arranged in order: kings, princes, grandees of Spain, dukes, marquises, counts, viscounts, barons, etc., and if they speak of another person, in order to be sure beforehand that he is decent and respectable, run to see if he is included in the book of "class" or not. A man's true personality, which is his unique class, does not count. I have also held in my hand an album belonging to a haughty young lady of Madrid, who arranged the portraits of her family in the following order: The eternal Father, Jesus Christ, The Pope, King Alfonso XIII, the girl's father, the Virgin, Queen Christina, the girl's mother, and the girl. Every Spanish or European noblewoman with a more or less valuable and elaborate crown (for crowns, too, have relative value) believes that on the day of the Last Judgment, when she arrives before God late, her cook being in her proper place already because she has always gotten up early, will say to her, "Madame, please go first." And they furthermore believe that God will be perfectly satisfied.

Into this capricious and nonsensical ignorance we find that both so-called aristocrats and democrats have fallen in Spain. It is the cynically religious notion of "classes" that all classes cherish.

4

The disdain for a human being, an artist, a scientist, or a poet for being an aristocrat, for being the friend and lover of beauty, religious or not, which occurs in Spain, in Europe, in Hispano–America (and I do not know to what extent in these United States, too) a strange, inconceivable paradox, above all when the arrogant one is a so-called democrat, and it happens often enough. And what a paradox it is to disdain the best or the desire for the best. And in the name of what? What indeed is superior to the love and the glorification of beautiful things, the love and the

glorification of everything worthy to be loved and glorified?
The great ones of the world, in both ancient and modern
times, have loved and glorified the beauty of life in all of its
aspects: a Leonardo, a St. John of the Cross, a Mozart, a Goethe,
a Keats, a Beethoven, a Bécquer, a Chopin, a Baudelaire, an
Emily Dickinson, a Debussy, and others who with pro-
foundly esthetic values illuminate our life through the glory of
the antique civilizations, Chinese, Indian, Greek. And what is it
that these supposedly cultivated "friends of the people" want an
Einstein, for example, to do today to be worthy of them? Ein-
stein is an indubitable aristocrat of science and of art, of science
for science and of art for art for all, for the great majority—a
pure mathematician and a true democrat. He has always been
on the side of justice. But does he have to leave his pure mathe-
matics to write mathematics at so much per penny to be worthy of
the people and to be understood by them? Instead of raising har-
mony to the heights with his burning enthusiasm, would a
Toscanini do better by playing mediocre works for the masses or
by introducing an accordion soloist into his orchestra? Would
not this be offending the public most profoundly? Would it not
be presuming that the people can never attain to science, art, or
the highest beauty and besides, for this reason, will perhaps do
away with it?

In fact the best, the most aristocratic poet or scientist ought to
be, by virtue of his culture and cultivation, the man of the finest
feelings. It is also clear that science and poetry can coincide with
false aristocracy or democracy and even occur under worse con-
ditions. But poetry, art, science, pure aristocrats will never be a
part of these conditions for any logical reason but only through
some monstrous exception. The conventional aristocrat, as an in-
herent concomitant of his social advantages, fortunately does not
have the gift of security in truth or beauty, the conventional
democrat, just as little, even though he, in his way, boasts of it,
They are both accustomed to value as art, science, or poetry, con-

ventional and rather slick forms of expression, practised by the so-called bourgeoisie. All one has to do is to see the books, the periodicals of such people. For example they take for poetry the farcical spectacle of the so-called "juegos florales" [official poetry contests], or the so-called national festivals, gastronomic love verses, ostentatious and materialistic ritual or vulgar theosophy for religion. As science they accept vulgarization, as art painted moralizing, moralizing which they do not even practice. For what do they think, if these aristocracies and bourgeoisies do think, of a Fray Luís de León to whom they gave prison and disgrace in his time because he aspired to beauty and truth and defended them to the end? And what does conventional democracy think of him?

The Spanish bourgeoisie and aristocracy have always imprisoned the people and deprived them of everything, the people which understood better than they a St. John of the Cross, and all the poets, aristocrats through being poets, and authentic friends of the people. And the so-called democrats, the so-called friends of the people, how do they behave toward poetry? I know a communist party secretary, an excellent person and a good friend of mine, who believes with honest commiseration that flowers, music, and birds are the concern of esthetes, of aristocrats. Delicacy, enthusiasm for the beautiful, for the esthetic, is a knotty problem for more or less communist democrats. A man, if he has to be a man among men and among their women, must not be able to tell a rose from a canary or a star; this is appropriate to women and decadents, or better yet, lunatics. Nature is therefore decadent because it produces flowers, stars, and birds. The man among men, when he finishes his daily toil, or when he rests, can not sit down to contemplate the sun, the clouds, or the moon, he must cover up his nose so as not to smell jasmine, his ears so as not to hear a green finch. If he is to be of the people and a friend of the people, he has to go and get drunk in the tavern or exhibit himself in a cabaret. Consequently it follows that the people confounds false aristocracy with the true and disdains, at the same time, the rich idler who lives on human blood and the refined and dedicated worker.

In Havana I heard a professed Cuban popularist, a man of sausages and wine dregs, shriek against a poet who was, alas, helping him to preside over a more or less popular function, because the poet sometimes wrote about the moon. This cannibalistic democrat no doubt did not know, among other things, that almost all the fine songs of the beautiful Spanish people are full of the moon or the stars:

> "Ah, glittering moon,
> All night you shine upon me
> As you come and go,
> All night you shine upon me."

Yes, that dark and clawed fanatic believed that the moon and the loaf of bread were incompatible, or worse, that the moon was the loaf of bread and a piece of meat.

But it is still sadder that exceptional people think this way, people who handle these dubious classes. In 1914, José Ortega y Gasset, our illustrious, liberal philosopher (in a lecture which he gave at the Atheneum of Madrid when the "great war" began, now just one more war) asked how it was possible that a Spanish poet, a good friend of his and well known, could publish a book in which he spoke among other deaths of that of a dog when so many men were dying in the trenches? The writer answered him as they left, by saying that what he had done in the lecture was to climb on top of the dead dog and the human poet in order to achieve a facile success with the "public," and that if all men were capable of writing an elegy on the death of their dogs, in peace or in war, there would be no war in the world. "I suppose," he added, "that you nowadays do not look at the stars, or smell the flowers, or kiss your children, or listen to the birds, and that you have ordered your house dog done away with."

How different was the Spanish child, a refugee from this other war who, as he passed by Havana in the *Mexique,* said to me compassionately, "In Málaga the Italians, when we were retreating, machine-gunned the donkeys too." Ortega y Gasset, who fundamentally possesses true aristocracy together with some rudeness, has always paraded the false aristocracy out of co-quetry or a desire to be fashionable and this perhaps explains the fickleness of his ideas and his life.

And what about the mixture of the so-called aristocrat and the so-called democrat in a single body? A large book now circu-lates here and there (because its author has written and pub-lished for propaganda purposes in the United States) a large book charged with passion, hatred, falsehood, fraud, and spite, whose author, a bourgeois from Madrid with pretentions to false aristocracy whom I know well, elevates her lineage in order to give her patronizing of the people an air and also by means of it to make the poor Spanish people important. This is a matter of a labyrinthine exploitation, of a varied mine of aristocracy, bour-geoisie, democracy, communism, and anarchy, all summed up in the author, which has to be exploited. What a sad idea this wretched Spanish woman has of what constitutes communism and what constitutes aristocracy! What an exhibition does she make of one and the other! This false communist aristocracy, a new Spanish class, makes itself available for everything: it is a bank, a lottery, an auction. And is this the Spain which democ-racy and communism was preparing for us in contrast to the one the bourgeoisie and the aristocracy prepared for us. Conse-quently I, a free man, wish to have nothing to do with any of them, either the false imperialist or the false communist Spain. In any case we all know that imperialist one lives in a hollow and gaudy lie which is rhetorical literature and who can believe that the other one is the simple, complete truth, poetry? I detest the dictatorship of fascism and communism. My superior man is neither a dictator nor an imperialist but a human being filled with love, delicacy and enthusiasm who is, in himself, all of superior humanity.

5

There is no doubt then that the old aristocracy of the old world has to rise to the profundity of the people and that the people has to rise to the background of the aristocracy. In these United States of yours (I return to the beginning for my ending) democracy can exist because there is neither a false hereditary people or aristocracy. It is perhaps the only country in the world where this is possible and for this reason we free Spaniards feel at home in it. Our Don Quixote in his sad and noble dementia wanted to bring about the two ascents mentioned above and was apparently defeated by his own Spain. St. Teresa, younger sister of Don Quixote, on the contrary, being acquainted with a more terrestrial and celestial world, or perhaps being a woman, knew how to blend the two in terms of the conditions of her time and, concretely, in religious communities. Did St. Teresa triumph? Is the religious Spain of today hers? Did not an aristocrat push St. Teresa into the river when they both met on a bridge? Religious communities were and are, since they renew themselves very little, a form of communism which is partially aristocratic; communism by virtue of their economic unity and their abolition of the personality, aristocratic in their renunciation and aspiration. We must not forget that Christianity was a true communism in its beginning, "Sufficient unto the day are the evils thereof," and its apostles were people who were rising, that is men aspiring to aristocracy. It was a communal religion for the poor and the slaves, a celestial mirage for people oppressed on earth, and we see by certain signs it was certainly a resigned aristocracy. Then, in the shadow of the Roman church, the privileged classes made it into a religion for the "privileged" classes. I do not know what Catholicism is in the United States but in Europe it is on the whole a false Christianity, choking the ideal essence of Christ in its extravagant and rhetorical ritual.

The military community is another species of relative aristocracy and its equivalence with the Catholic deprives it of popular prestige. I have little faith in militarism. But, tolerant of alien ideas as I am, I do not doubt that a cultured and cultivated soldier can be a true aristocrat. And what advantages would follow in the world if the military blades, like those of lilies, were blades of peace. But whoever treated his sword thus would be shot for being a poet, an aristocrat. As they would shoot me if they should hear what I am saying, these so-called aristocrats, democrats, soldiers and priests of Spain, with certain exceptions.

Always and in everything one must end with poetry which is the unequaled expression of aristocracy, seeing that it is the interpretation of the not-necessarily religious, ineffable, without rewards and punishments, that is to say the completely ineffable, universal and absolute. The poet in the name of the authentic good is the greatest enemy of the worst, of the false; he is, since he is a pure aristocrat, the pure popularist. The poet has never forgotten that what is really the worst is injustice, hunger, poverty, in one sense or the other, vulgarization, hatred, and crime.

Let us not, we Spaniards, we Europeans, do any more damage to society by our usual incomprehension of these mistaken concepts. Let us not accept or inflate a democracy which means in the noble moral sense, collective disgrace, let us not use this label as an ideological argument for accepting a definite evil. Is it possible that we, who love the people should wish it to go on being the plebians, population, masses, instead of a people and that it should rule in this condition as it now rules and governs us? No, let us not play with the word democracy as a symbol of the uncultivated masses, or with the word aristocracy as the symbol of another sort of more uncultivated masses, let us not remain among the intermediate masses involved in a stupid interplay between the other two evil masses. Let us not contribute our comfort to an uncomfortable permanence. More than a democrat, I want to be a brother to the people, brother to the people in a hopeful state of transition. I want to have nothing to do with these fakers, called in Europe and Spain, "defenders of the people," who seem to wish only to keep the people eternally uncultured to justify a political policy or a manner of living, and I shall always be against them, not only in my own name but in that of the people, dedicating my thoughts and my feelings to the latter and transmitting to it, and transmitting to myself at the same time, its desire for a unique and definitive life.

I, a man born in the old world, always aspiring to the ideal world, and living now, I do not know how transitorily or permanently in the new world (depending on what the old world will say), I wish to be an aristocrat, to reach the best, to help integrate a better society; I am anxious that the so-called people and the so-called "classes" should fuse their separate masses by means of a communicating fire in an organism full of understanding and love. And in this fusion, needless to say, we must lose the middle class (well named for its mediocrity) the worst of all names, and I hope that this "class" does not also take form by mistake either in the United States.

Thus all our beautiful, sad, grotesque, joyful, lamentable, heroic, terrible, sweet, sublime humanity will in itself one day be fashioned in the likeness of a splendid illusion which, like poetry, can never be quit of the all, and, like poetry, shall have sufficient reality. And let us contribute our fervent enthusiasm as poets of the human future to this hope of union; let us do it every day through our joyful labor and with our better selves. We must not hope for this unity from the political fantasms which rule us now, taking advantage of our facile hopes, nor must we, like mystics turned outward, seek it in an obscure invisible power, master of forgetfulness, created by the uncultivated masses and made use of by the uncultivated privileged masses, the power to reward or punish which serves to alleviate our weariness, this power, a being dedicated in itself and for us to an eternal injustice.

From the University of Miami Hispanic-American Studies, No. 2/1941

POETRY AND LITERATURE

Written poetry seems to me, continues to seem to me, to be a form of expression (like the musical form, etc.) of the ineffable, of that which can not be said, if the redundancy can be pardoned, of what is unrealizable. Literature is the expression of the concrete, what can be expressed, something attainable. And since I believe spirit is immanent ineffability, immanence of the ineffable, it is clear to me that written poetry inevitably has to be spiritual and that literature does not necessarily have to be or even to try to be, for its destiny is different.

The states of contemplation of the ineffable are pantheism, mysticism (I do not exactly refer to the religious), love, that is, communication, discovery, entry into nature and spirit, into the visible and invisible reality, into the double everything, whose absolute shadow is a double nothing. Man is disposed toward these states by feeling, thought, and accent. The result, mute or written, is universal emotion (let us drop that little word "cosmic" which is so fashionable).

Poetry will then be an intimate, profound (lofty and deep) fusion within ourselves, thanks to our contemplation and creation, of the real, which we believe we know, and the transcendental which we believe we do not know. It will be, at the same time, our imponderable loss and gain. And, since this innermost phenomenon which sets our being in motion is inevitably rhythmical, like every enthusiasm, poetry as we ourselves and others express, it will be inevitably rhythmical, musical rather than pictorial, seeing that in music and the dance, dynamic ecstasy, the eyes are not turned outward but within oneself. For this reason authentic dancers, poets of absolute rhythm, Davids, say that to dance you have to look within. As consciousness does not work in such a state of complete dynamic ecstasy, in such a presence in absence, poetry is necessarily intuitive and by the same token elemental, simple, for it is only one, object and subject of its creation and its contemplation and these things do not call for unnecessary adornment. In reality the poet, when mute or when writing, is an abstract dancer, and if he writes, it is out of an everyday weakness, for to be truly consistent he ought not to write. He who ought to write is the literary man.

Literature depends, like necessary writing, upon the eyes just as painting does and will be decorative, ingenious, external, because it is not being created but compared, commented on, copied. Literature is translation, poetry original. If poetry deals with profound emotions, literature deals with the superficial ones, if poetry is instinctive and by the same token terse, easy, like a flower or fruit, if it is all of one piece, literature, dominated, obsessed as it is by the external which it has to incorporate, will be labored, forced, juxtaposed, baroque.

I believe that the arts (and the sciences, too) are divided into creative arts and imitative arts. The creative ones are, for example, the dance, poetry and written metaphysics, metaphysics being more art than science; the imitative arts, for example, are painting, sculpture, the novel. The theater can be a creative art if it is abstract, imitative if it is anecdotal.

Written poetry, like other creative arts, is always natural, however perfect it may be, or rather it is perfect and complete because it is natural. Literature, however perfect it may be, is always artificial, the more artificial, the more perfect. Through literature it is possible to arrive at a relative beauty but poetry is far beyond relative beauty and its expression aspires to absolute beauty. We never arrive at its domain, unless it makes contact with us, unless it comes to us, unless we merit it because of our restlessness and enthusiasm. Consequently it is maintained in the platonic style that the poet is a medium, one possessed of an attainable god. I do not think the poet needs any god; he can be a medium indeed since the god in man is truth, a medium which man has invented or confirmed to be able to communicate with or to understand the absolute. Thus god can be a poet or a poet can be god. And this is not saying that the universe of the poet is less than that of the god, if we assume that God created the visible and reserves the invisible for himself or as a reward for us and that the poet dispenses with the visible and tarries in the invisible giving what he finds to whomever may desire it.

Because poetry "is" in itself, it is nothing and everything, before and after; action, verb, creation and therefore poetry, beauty and all the rest. Pretentious literature must be content to reach a mirrored beauty by a complicated rite, literature can secure the gleam of poetry in its glass when it is copied from poetic writing by the latter's imitators.

In written poetry one does not, it is clear one can not ever arrive completely. For this reason true poetic writing can not be perfect or aspire to be. A novel, a statue can be perfect, can be finished, terminated, by that I mean dead. And for this reason, too, true poets do not make much concession in communication to the regular written "forms" but nearly always, or at least when they are at their best, use invented forms or convert the rigid forms of the literary men into flexible forms. In this matter of so-called form, literature has made writing complicated. And the poets, the nightingales, blind to the external, sometimes fall into formal vices, the trap prepared by the envious and covetous literary men and the malignant critics and then they, too, make literature, converting their grace into disgrace.

Between poetry and literature there is the same distance, as, for example, between love and appetite, sensuality and sexuality, word and wordiness, since literature is boasting, exaggeration, donjuanism, and creates its emphasis in terms of its atmosphere and its manner from fashion. Poetry can only become intricate, difficult, when its rhetoric is not the product of the idea, the spirit, but of the word, the pen. Consequently literature has invented rhetoric, which is a juggler's game of clever writers. The poet at times also makes a fool of himself and, a prey to the aforementioned vice, plays the literary men's games, achieving more miracles than they. The literary man scarcely ever makes a mistake, he nearly always catches the plates he has tossed into the air and if one falls, it falls on someone else's head. The poet customarily loses some plates but they do not fall on any head, they are lost in the infinite because he is a good friend of space.

There are enough pedantic juggling rhetoricians who imagine that by means of conceptual science, which is their limited treasure, for bait and as a lure, they have done no less than catch poetry, possessing it body and soul, that they have found the heart, the core, and that they have "written" it, "realized" it. And fortunately poetry is never "realized" by everyone, it always escapes and the true poet, who is usually an honorable person because he has the habit of living with truth, knows how to let it escape since the state of poetic grace, the dynamic ecstasy, the rhythmic, drunken rapture, the unutterable, palpitating miracle from which the essential accent arises, is indeed a form of flight, a passionate form of liberty.

Nothing is further from poetry and love, from poetry written with love, than more or less rotund literature, more or less ably constructed, with poetic pretensions to complete love. The literary man usually makes fun of the emotion in profound movement, he wants to be showily dynamic and says that the poet is a poor, useless being since he scarcely moves, and other people, dazzled by the glittering farce, by the winning of ready, clinking cash, also say that the enraptured poet, the nightingale-man is a poor, useless being.

Authentic poetry is known by its profound emotion, by its full, deep tide. By its intuitive metaphysics. When it is said that a certain conceptual literary man is more profound than a certain subjective poet, he who says it forgets that there are many kinds of profundity: that of concept, that of image, that of thought, that of feeling, etc. It is like saying that a watermelon is more profound than a rose. The incomparable can not be compared. Literature can be very rich in profundity of style, in metaphor, in concept, in cerebral physique, but there is a more profound profundity, the unfathomable profundity, the genuine sense of what is bottomless.

As literature enjoys such a pompous ascendancy and thus a relative aristocracy, it has blazoned the parrot and the peacock on its complicated crest. Poetry, inasmuch as the simple poet always begins with himself and is the real progressive aristocrat perhaps without realizing it, it bears in its soul which has no escutcheon, the solitary nightingale freed from its escutcheoned cage; the nightingale which, according to a humorous and sensitive poet (and may I be forgiven this one quote from someone else, I, who am no friend to walking on borrowed feet) was prior to the act and the verb, was in the beginning.

It is not possible to continue with this topic which is moreover endless, and I am going to sum up what I have said up to now in a few words, those with which I must always end when I speak of poetry: literature is a state of culture, poetry a state of grace, before and after culture.

From the University of Miami Hispanic-American Studies/Number 2., 1941

7

1936-1956/From the latest books written in America

OFFENDED DOVE

By the rocks I hear you sighing
As you tread backward.
Arise, I am not hard,
Lost dove.

Have they clipped your concave wings?
You can not open them?
Come, I am not sluggish,
Suffering dove!

With your eyes you arrest the sun
And you halt the breeze.

Come, I am not tardy,
Exhausted dove!

In my mouth I keep your thirst,
Your thirst that is mine.
Enter, I am not dried up,
Offended dove.

Canciónes de la Florida / 1936-1942

THE BIRDS FROM I KNOW WHERE

All through the night
The birds have been
Singing me their colors.

(Not the colors
Of their morning wings
With the newness of suns.

Not the colors
Of their evening breasts
In the embers of suns.

Not the colors of
Their daily beaks
Which are extinguished by night
As the familiar colors

Of leaves and flowers
Are extinguished.)

Other colors.
The first paradise
Which man lost wholly.
The paradise
Which the birds and the flowers
Know immensely.

Flowers and birds
In perfumed coming and going,
Flying all over the earth.

Other colors,
The unchanging paradise
That man traverses in dreams.

All through the night
The birds have been
Singing me their colors.

Other colors
That they have in their other world
That emerge at nighttime.

Some colors
That I have seen when wide awake
And well I know where they are.

I know where the birds
Have come from
To sing to me in the nighttime.

I know where they come from,
Traversing winds and waves
To sing me their colors.

Canciónes de la Florida/1936-1942

SECOND FRAGMENT

(*Sung*)

"And to remember why I have lived," I come to you, Hudson River, from my sea. "Sweet as this light was love . . ." "And below the George Washington Bridge (the bridge with the most of this New York) passes the yellow field of my childhood." Childhood, child I become again and am, lost, however grownup, in what is larger. Unawaited legend, "Sweet as light is love," and this New York is like Moguer, is like Seville, is like Madrid. The wind is stronger than I am on the corner of Broadway just as on Pneumonia Corner of my Rascón Street, and I keep the door open where I live, letting the sun in. "Love was as sweet as this sun." I met somebody, I laughed at him and I went up once more to the provisional corner of my solitude and silence, just the same on the ninth floor in the sun as in the low room of my street and sky. "Love is as sweet as this sun." Windows with pictures by Murillo stared at me. On the wire in the sky, the universal sparrow sang, the sparrow and I were singing, we talked and I heard the voice of a woman in the wind of the world. What a corner indeed for my fantasy to take place in! The sun burned the south of my corner and in the waning moon of the matting my illusion gradually grew, seeking to fly from the gilded poverty. "And below the George

Washington Bridge, the friendliest bridge in New York, runs the guilded countryside of my childhood . . ." Surfeited, I went down to the street, the wind opened my clothes, my heart; I saw good faces. The green poplars in the garden of St. John the Divine were from Madrid; I spoke with a dog and a cat in Spanish, and the choirboys were singing in the eternal language, like that of paradise and the moon, along with the bells of St. John's cathedral in the rays of the live midday sun, where the sky floated, making a violet and gold harmony, an ideal rainbow that rose and fell. . . . "Love was as sweet as the sun." I went out on Amsterdam Avenue, the moon was there (Morningside); the air was so pure, cold, no cool, cool, the life of a spring night came to me in it, and the sun was inside the moon and my body, the present sun, the sun which would nevermore leave my bones lonely, sun in blood and in *him*. And, absently singing, I entered the foliage of the night and the river which, along with the sun, slid under the George Washington Bridge toward my Spain, through my east, to my Madrid in the east, a sun already dead but alive, a sun present but absent, a sun embered with live carmine, a live sun in the greenery, a live carmine sun in the already dark greenery, a sun in the darkness already moon, a sun in the great, carmine moon, a sun of new glory, new in another east, a sun of beautiful love and labor, a sun like love . . . "Sweet as this sun was love."

Espacio/1941-1942-1954

THE BEST NIGHT

As I pacified him
And in grace he was sleeping,
The nightingale sang of it,
The night and the sunrise.

The bluest stars
Descended to his bedside,
Waters of all colors
Approached him from far away.

"Do you hear the nightingale?" "Yes,"
In a faraway voice he answered me,
In a nearby voice he said to me,
"Yes, I hear, what a pretty song!"

Was he not bound to find it pretty,
If, his soul and body divided,
Going and coming from me,
He was with it and absent from it?

If, lost in his verity,
If, with his verity gained,
He was sighing and smiling
His losses and gains?

Was he not bound to find it pretty
If, with his face already covered,
He heard it from his finality,
From his everything and his nothing?

Romances de Coral Gables / 1939-1942

TREES MEN

Yesterday afternoon
I returned with the clouds
That were entering low rosebushes,
(A great, round tenderness)
Among the steadfast tree trunks.

The solitude was tender
And the silence inexhaustible.
I stood still like a tree
And I heard the trees talking.

The lonely bird fled away
From so secret a halting place,
Only I could remain
Among the last of the roses.

I did not want to return
To myself for fear of offending
The trees, that were all so similar,
By a tree that was different.

The trees had quite forgotten
My shape of wanderer
And, with my shape forgotten,
I heard the trees talking.

I waited for the starlight.
In a flight of soft radiance
I went down to the edge
With the moon already in the sky.

Already, as I went down,
I saw the trees look at me.

They were aware of everything
And I found it hard to leave them.

Among mother-of-pearl clouds
I heard them talking
About me, in a gentle murmur.
And how could I disappoint them?

How could I say to them, no,
I was only a passerby
And they should not talk to me about me?
I did not want to betray them.

And then quite late yesterday evening
I heard myself talk to the trees.

Romances de Coral Gables/1939-1942

THE MOST FAITHFUL

The sad cocks were crowing
As a sign of destiny.
A man rose to his feet
And dreamless, looked into the abyss.

But before the reddish light
Trimmed down the broken pine tree,
One who was quite different
Went on lying down the same way.

The other who came spoke,
The submissive animal came.
A smoke had a perfume of woman
The door opened the road.

The bird, the wheat, the water
All rose up in the cleanness,
But one did not rise up at all,
The one that was quite different.

(Where did he greet the bird,
Where did he hear the streamlet,
Whence did he see himself
Lying down like another wheatear?)

But one did not rise up at all,
The one who was quite different,
But he did not rise up,
The one who was there in his place.

(Where, he who is lying down
Is standing, like a river,
Thirst a fact, water a fact,
A single faithful reflection,)

But he did not rise up at all,
The one who was already steadfast,
One, he who was already in him,
One, the definitely faithful.

Romances de Coral Gables/1939-1942

HEROIC REASON

Anyone who progresses in one discipline (poetry, for example, religion, art, or science, etc.) will inevitably progress in all others even though he may not consider them individually to be his. When he wishes to relate another discipline to his own, he will reach it at an equivalent level. He will not, perhaps, be so well versed in the other as in his own but he will make similar demands upon it. For him, the progressive man, all the world will be a daily delightful, uphill climb, that great uphill climb which he can surmount with ease and grace because his own progress will have been a universal progress. The progressive individual propels the world onward without setting out to do so. This has been my opinion from my youth and from my earliest youth I have continued to substantiate it.

A progressive poet, for example, one who is renewed and up-to-date, is so primarily by means of his spirit, never by means of his artistic or scientific medium, nor through the medium upon which he works with his hands, never through his media. Change can take place through the medium but horizontally, not upward. The poet's aim is to rise. Technology can assure physical progress but it will not continue beyond this. A poet can sing marvellously, with unsurpassable virtuosity, an everyday, carnal act of love, just as he could sing the phenomenon of digestion but this in itself alone, as a fact, an anecdote without any relation to other intellectual, spiritual, or ideal phenomena, brings no credit to poetry.

If a man can not assert himself by means of his own medium or by means of alien media, because all is possible through fantasy, he will have difficulty in asserting his creativity by means of a universal medium or his own medium. A poet whose only vocation is the quotidian realism of our life, without ambition concerning things existent or non-existent created by his electric moral insight, without at least magic realism, can never be new. ("Actual means classic which means eternal," says a Spanish aphorism). And the poet always has to be new because novelty is continuation and it is difficult to conceive permanence without the present. Perpetuity, even if it extend in all directions, unless it is this substantive or adjective which has been made of it, can not be old nor conceive itself as old and for this reason eternity, figuratively stated, is what never grows old. The poet is an inner and outer progress through given time and space. And he who conceives time or eternity as old is he who has no consciousness of his own time or of his own attainable eternity, he who does not conceive his immanence, he who does not take into account or understand his destiny. A poet, merely traditional in spirit or form, a poet who merely looks backward, can be good, and enjoyed as good, but he does not fulfill his light-giving task, he does not pass on his own torch from day to day within himself or to others. The myth of return of eternal youth, of springtime, is that of poetry itself.

And if life were not aspiration toward permanence, it would die in the act, realism would kill true life. For this reason we see so many dead satisfied to be dead, satisfied with their own death, the ones who never had the desire to get outside of themselves, to progress in themselves or in others. To be truly alive, to revitalize oneself, to be forever new, one must necessarily be so primarily through an inborn instinct for the spiritual or the ideal and, of course, through daily cultivation as well; to lack all this is to be second-rate. The spirit is immanency in motion and all the spirit conceives as life has to be movement, becoming, a continual being like the surf or the waves of the sea, forever new without leaving its waters or its beaches, and new because its waves change continually, because it is movement, and forward movement. The poet of the spirit, he who understands all men and understands himself (through a complete inner illumination which transcends and makes the medium transcendent) is the only man who sees, orders, and controls every instant of life.

In these recent times humanity has become excessively realistic, that is to say it has aged, lost its enduringness, its eternalness, its timelessness. The political man, he of the *polis,* the city of the world, who ought to be a man of the most exemplary spirit, considering that he has to administer the material and moral progress of his country, more or less in millennia, has not been fulfilling his task. This, which could happen in other epochs is already unattainable in ours. Man was a realist in a cramped, shrunken, mistaken, decentralized world, a world in which not only time and space were shrunken, as they are to a much greater extent in our present world, but shrunken in inner genius. Neither the world nor the politician understood each other. At the beginning of the great catastrophe which for twelve years has been driving men mad, when a country (to which I feel so close that I do not wish to and can not exhibit it naked and bloody) was the first to be plunged in darkness by the mistakes of the realistic politicians of the whole world, an English paralytic, a mistaken retrograde person, a stagnant realist with a rotten soul, stated from his island that the great struggle which was beginning was an economic war and that it had to be considered a political deal since he considered politics to be a cut and dried business enterprise. This disgraced and disgraceful man was much deader then than he is today, now that he is under the earth and his death serves merely to record his error. He spoke, in his island, of death like a skeleton without eternity and he wished to condemn the whole world to a death without eternity.

I repeat continually that the political man seems to me to be the administrator of a people, a provisional administrator, a progressive executor, a tutor as long as the people cannot administer itself, and this citizen should never for a single moment of his life forget that what he has to administer is not only bread and water but, above all, the spirit of the people, and that a good administrator must be always alert to progressive development of and for the administered, and that he has to live always in the present if he really wants them to prosper, and I do not say live in the future because perhaps he could not endure disequilibrium and such living in the future is the task of poets, precursors of the politicians. To administer is not to repress the administered, nor to keep them in a vulgar, everyday, standardized condition even though the administration may be honest. It is to keep the administered prospering in all senses and in all directions in a realizable unity based on fraternal relationships with the rest of the world. Like the bread and water, the spirit is nourishment recreated from itself, an eternal phoenix, for the spirit is more alive with itself the more it works with itself, the more it cultivates itself. We are one with that which nourishes us and we convert our nourishment into ourselves, into men. Water, bread, and the spirit are always the same but can be always renewed through us, for us, and for others. A true political program which synthesizes the drives of the true society, a political program which feeds its people with material and ideal nourishment whose proper administration can foster the administered, has to be progressive and new, as poetry, its precursor, states and announces in advance.

In another lecture I have most insistently said that the supreme goal of man, a universal aristocracy, a universal and conscious aristocracy, is the goal of the so-called general progressive democracy. Since the beginning of the great war, in this great epoch in which we live, great because of the heights and depths in it (and I refer as much to the first world war as to the second which still goes on, and to the third in whose dark shadow we all live in horror), we hear every day, talking, shrieking, howling about democracy, but democracy is discussed or shouted about as a generally recognized phenomenon, without isolating it or clarifying it with a sufficient definition, perhaps as a result of ignorance or because there is no wish to unmask the deception which has been imposed and is tolerated. We talk about democracy more and more rapidly without convincing any conscious person of any sort of concept of what it is, without paying enough attention to it, without investigating its possibilities. Democracy is talked about as if it were an adjective not a substantive; to sum up, democracy is talked about without the love and respect which inspires confidence. And it seems to me because of this lack of respect, of confidence and understanding, of love for democracy, as consciousness, and for those with whom we discuss it, the general response is not that of assent or, when it is necessary, of heroism, that disposition toward the heroic which we would feel for any professional, scientific, religious, or artistic ideal. Thus it was noticeable in the United States of North America, and I noticed it when there, that the boys who had to go to Europe did not know why and did not feel heroic because they were not convinced that they had an ideal to defend with their lives. They were right. And as for those boys' girls, who were having a wonderful time while their boys fought, died and hoped, not knowing why or for what, I remember having read on various occasions that some of these girls, who were admonished for their insolence, answered that if they could not have all the liberty they wanted, then for what liberty and for what sort of democracy were their boys fighting and getting killed? And what else could they have said after hearing the version of democracy left them by that defunct Englishman of whom I spoke before? Today some of those boys, after their life and death struggle, have come to the point, like conscientious carpenters, of reconstructing what they had destroyed, unconsciously obeying a more or less blind sense of order. This at least is my hope.

With all possible respect for contrary opinions, I am going to cite an example. If abstract ideas can offend no one, is it not possible to criticize their application without being a propagandist? And I am in no sense a propagandist, I am a critic. English democracy, the European type of democracy, and I do not know if at any time it could have been in agreement with its epoch, does it go on being a progressive democracy in relation to its time? Is it a democracy which has renewed, improved, and aristocratized the Englishman morally and also the man who has been administered by the Englishman all over the world, or is it a static democracy, that is, a senseless one, since democracy is no more than a pathway, an ascent? Is it not a democracy without complete consciousness, which has no possibilities of spiritual life, of superior cultivation in time and space? After this current phenomenon of human disturbance, which has gone on for many years, if once and for all everything comes to a halt at something convincing, if it terminates with anyone reaching an adequate truth, even if the truth should be temporary, what sort of democracy would convince the world; supposing that he who has it most in his power to do so should help the world to gain it, to gain it for itself, which is what the world ought to be doing, and is what I wish for and, I suppose, all forward-looking democrats wish for? Can arbitrary, historical colonialism, for example, possibly go on being what it still is, what it has been allowed to be through imperial indolence and malevolence of whatever color? Will the subjugated world suddenly become a world of the living or else will it, with so many wordy epigrams on its forehead, go on being a world of the dead? Will it administer the peoples in progressive prosperity, will it bring them to their centers, I mean to the center of noble and cultivated human ambition? Will the word "colonialism" go on signifying something, will it have weight, volume, something which is not merely historical?

Every country should realize that its turn at world domination, domination because its rights coincided more or less with the character or progress of the epoch, must terminate with the change brought about by this progress. Spain dominated the world in the centuries of adventure, France in the centuries of social development, England in those of imperialism because it was an island and knew how to make use of the invention of steam. But now, whatever new inventions may come, the universal consciousness, admittedly or not, knows that imperialism has ended in our world, there is no longer any doubt about it. Though our epoch may seem terrible to us, we should be happy to live or die in it since we see it open on a new era and it signifies the obliteration of imperialism which is like a magnified feudalism, only much worse, for it is as if the individual feudal lords had swelled into individual feudal countries. In my opinion the only way in which a country can rule others, whose progressive destinies are not yet achieved, in the only noble sense of the word (I am thinking of moral influence), is by example and in no way except by example, for this is the standard by which the others' aspirations can be measured, favorably or unfavorably.

And as for North American democracy, more advanced as it doubtless is in everyday matters than the English democracy, is it sufficient to produce a superior consciousness?

The ideal example. Let us consider this. Man, human society, can never reach an absolute goal, both can always be more than they are, and ought to be, since every augmentation carries new perspectives with it, because illusion, unreal though it is, is the mirror of a reality because its outcome, in the material sense, will be its goal and it is clear that we shall always continue to walk around our orbit as long as a cosmic catastrophe inside or outside it does not put an end to us or our concerns. Society and man are simply and always progression, provisionality, becoming, the present, and this is man's great strength, to be always in the present and to know that he always can be if he succeeds in feeling this strength and in feeling himself within it. It is like an eager journey to a place awaiting us full of beauty and destiny. We see a light at the end of the horizon, a glow in the air like an explosion, something that subdues us like a sudden truth. And we arrive, hoping and enjoying, almost without knowing it, yet we do not arrive at the place, because we neither know whether we arrive or not, since we always paint this mirage with a new color as we grow and perhaps fantastically transcend it. We are already more than the place of illusion at which we have arrived.

The virtue of the attraction is likewise forever new, what attracts does so with ever renewed magnetism. We can not reach the ideal because we, too, are always new whether we understand it or not, whether we make use of it or not. Thus we can never treat the social ideal as a limit but rather as a state of transition. The civilizations which have invented limits were or are decadent civilizations. The only thing superior to man is his renewal. For that reason the ideal only exists at our side or rather within us; it can not exist as a block of stone, as idealistic statuary but rather as an ever-transparent pillar of flame that flows in front of us; we are living, we go on living in its light and, at the same time, in the light that it throws in front of itself and us. This is man's great secret and the secret of his life and thus we can live when we are wholly absorbed in thinking and feeling, illuminated by ourselves, knowing that this thinking and feeling can change every day as do the illusions of a child.

And I arise every day with the illusions of a child, even when sickness sometimes mistreats me, because these illusions raise me to my wholesome islands of quality and they, with their sun, are what allow me to live. I do not cut my life up into days but my days into lives, each day, each hour, an entire life. And what a theatrical performance my own life presents for me even though at times my expression is melancholy, because expression can travel a pathway of qualities which melancholy embellishes.

Thus the concept of a definite heaven in any religion with a static eternity seems to me to be the same as a sea of motionless fossilized waves, a concept inferior to that of life in a state of ideal and real metamorphosis within our own paradise. I say that I believe in a progressive god, and that for me heaven is progress and poetry poetization; to poetize is to arrive, to come to be myself every day and with a new vision and a new expression of myself and of the world that I see, my world. When a man becomes enfeebled, his bones drop down, they drop down; and if his life has been progressive, the remaining exemplary bone is converted into supreme fertilizer, because I believe movement, emotion are the only things which can endure in themselves in any human work, beyond partisan criticism, pervading all the rest of it. This passing on of the torch from one to the other I, and from me to him who follows me, these stages in the beautiful career of light, without any other egoistic concept except that of the complete, superior life, are my permanent conception of life. Democracy which is nothing less than progressive politics of the whole man ought to be considered the creator of the complete, superior life with no personal egoism. The orbit of democracy consists in passing on political ideals, passing them on upward, when he who come behind (in reality he who goes ahead) already sees further than the vision of a single individual. Democracy is the renunciation of one in favor of other discontented travellers of the world, renunciation of the egoism of living apart in favor of living more advantageously for everyone and, when it is necessary, for those who are to come, the renunciation of the individual difference in favor of the whole organism's convincing superiority, in favor of a conviction of a more beautiful unity.

We frequently see people who call themselves democrats treat democracy like a theatrical performance, "what you see, what we are seeing," they say, "is democracy. And here we are in our orchestra box seat, or first, second, or third row, observing it on the stage and in the balcony, called by some, paradise." In any case those who say this participate, without friction, as in a theatre, rather than participating in the crowd with which they casually rub elbows, so that others can see that they are there looking on or observing, letting others put on or likewise observe the theatrical performance. This is what is commonly called politics. Or perhaps they are amateur actors, which is the worst of all, since they put on the comedy or the drama without really participating in it, without feeling it themselves, making mistakes, or else depending upon a prompter who reads without thinking unless, without thinking, a fall of the curtain kills them all off. These people, these frivolously vulgar actors, are those who divide life in general into a good or bad play depending on whether they have to pay more or less for their seats or for their costumes or depending upon whether they possess more or less money or more or less insolence with which to pay for their seat in life. Let us think of this, those of us who are seated here in our seats in life. When the act is over, many shake off the dust which may have fallen upon them and, knowing that they deceive themselves, go out thinking they have fulfilled their duty to others. They believe that by shutting themselves up in their houses they cut themselves off from the drama; but no, the drama is never cut off from itself nor, for that matter, from them. The drama continues through the stages of life like a greater or lesser nebula of human flesh and soul, circling its orbit around that which might have been. This is why the human drama sometimes takes on the appearance of a geological catastrophe as if men were rocks, waves, flames or hurricanes, as if man were suddenly the elemental being which he was in origin. It is because those who could give consciousness and vision to the lazy onlookers, that is the egoistical, critical spectators, leave them blind, without consciousness, since they know they are not being seen or understood. But the nebula has a consciousness, a nebulous consciousness, a consciousness of god in the nebula and feels and acts as nebula, and it struggles to progress, stumbling and falling in its orbit, because nothing can escape from the orbit without coming to a stop.

For years, years which seem like centuries, the world has been going through one of these catastrophic phases. The human nebula, disregarded by the egoistic spectator, has shown itself the same as in other times during the sinking of an Atlantis. Ibsen said, in a poem that I translated when I was nineteen, that the only true revolution he knew of was the universal flood because it was equalitarian and he begged that he be permitted to bring it about a second time by unloosing all the waters and he said that he would really finish everything with a torpedo under the ark. This is the anarchistic point of view of a lazy man and, without realizing it, one or another demented politician or poet in one way or another has tried it. And the fault has not lain with those Neronean amateurs or those Ibsenian or Nietzschean realists of world drama but in the egoistic spectator of the whole world, the man without universal human heroism, and I do not mean heroism of the combatant but that of clairvoyance, the spectator of the heroism of reason, of the reason or unreason of heroism, the dilettante of life who does not give way to reason and who keeps his consciousness like an object of luxury, a luxurious subject of which to speak over the radio to the human nebula which he wants to treat as an eternal nebula, a source for them. Or there are those who howl in epileptic attacks, with the gestures of circus lions and then have their pictures taken with a handkerchief sticking out of their breast pockets. We have seen in recent years that men of conscience, heroic in their material weakness, have given a moral example to men and countries with greater material strength and greater material territory. As always happens they were the vanguard, the sacrificial victims, the best who paid first. Fat men and fat countries, egoistic spectators, said to them, "You go ahead for we, the illustrious, giant democracies are here to back you up." And they fell, they fell as an example which perhaps was what was desired. And when the great materialism fell, too, because its foundation was not understanding but egoism, the fat ones had to take up the fallen example once more, they were forced to imitate those genuine weak heroes to be able to go on living, getting fatter and preparing for another catastrophe.

It is customary to consider foreign countries enemies because of the sole fact that they are strangers. The world is seen as a series of parcels alien to each other, more so in feelings than space, set off by different colors, those vague colors of ideas and flags. The world is like a map of antipathies, almost of hates, in which everyone picks the symbolic color of his difference. But in the world there is nothing really alien because it is all world and of the world, now so small and traversable that is all fits into one day. And how can anyone believe or be made to believe that it is so different or so alien? Neither countries nor races are strangers. It is all a question of façade; eyes are not strangers, nor ideas, the consciousness and physical essences of these races and nations can not and ought not to be so. Whether we wish it or not, humanity is universal man and woman who are seeking to love. Humanity exists in one point of space and could go on existing in a paradise (even though lost in the beginning) and humanity has a single limit, the best, not the best imposed in advance but the best achieved by experiment, the best within a voluntarily accepted liberty. Emotionally every man (each in his own way in relation to his fulfilled or to be fulfilled existence, with his fulfilled or to be fulfilled being) reaches out for the best that man can imagine, and this best we can learn from all men's illusions, even from those who seem most different or alien to us.

Language is perhaps the thing which most divides us but, to the extent that a stranger speaks our language, or we his, we are the same. Yet even as all are the same as we are when we speak the same language, we can all be more similar still by means of other like transformations. And not even the savage, moreover, is worse or different because of the fact of being a savage; indeed the civilized savage surpasses the innocent savage in every sense, inversely. We have all seen how many people supposedly alien from innocent savagery enjoy playing the primitive. In all primitive, savage countries we meet expressions of emotion and thought in beautiful form and it would be hard to improve on the artistic sensitivity of many savage countries, or those which are called savage, although they are not aware that they are, just as an animal shows us more affection than a man, with more common sense, unaware, poor fellow, that we characterize him as unreasoning. When many great civilized artists have approached or do approach decadence because of civilized preciosity they have always had to and have to return to the purity, the delicacy or the strength of their art, which is then called primitive. Only look at the Negroes in the field, the colors they wear, the movements they make, how they laugh, cry, and dance and you will see how nature accepts them in everything they do intentionally or accidentally. In contrast how very alien to nature the ridiculous civilization of the majority remains, the culture of the whitest civilization!

The highest form of human equality is expressed through feeling. It is possible that instinct cultivated by technical progress may be superior in a certain sense to instinct uncultivated except through immediate use. But the intelligence should never be used to make us feel superior to others, nor at the expense of others, nor to divide us from others through intelligence and understanding but rather to unite us all through understanding, through the acceptance of inner cultivation. The intelligence can not serve to separate us into races, colors, castes, or classes or above all into levels of culture, but rather to make us sympathize with everyone in every way we can. If our five senses are alike in all of us humans, how can we fail to resemble each other? We should wish to give everyone our chosen progress and not to hide or dissimulate it from those who seem to us pragmatic and not progressive; we ought to accept and humor the infantile tricks of their ingenuous ignorance or of their crude curiosity, as we do children, as we do children more ours, and we ought not to view them, as so many do through their caprices, as in a state of monstrous infancy which becomes more acceptable the closer they adapt themselves to us without knowing why.

It would be interesting to follow out this thought to see if what divides men may not be precisely the intelligence, the so-called ideas, ideas held for good or for evil, for a so-called good idea alienates a so-called evil man just as a so-called bad idea alienates a so-called good man. It appears that ideas, bad ideas, are what produce war among men and that feelings alone are what can be invoked to mitigate the cruelty of ideas. If asphyxiating gases are not used, it is in "honor" of feeling. Which means that feelings are superior to ideas, that we can easily reach others through the feelings and that consequently it is in ideology that we must learn to bring about a rapprochement. It seems evident that ideas are not in reality either bad or good any more than weapons or poisons; the bad or good derives from the ideologist who loses the ability to feel. Religions are good, actively good, when they are based on feeling more than on ideology and all religious decadence is generally theological, that is to say a vain intellectual explanation of religious sentiment which is susceptible of no other explanation than its own destiny. And so it is probable that the possibility of union among men may lie in the sciences, not in the arts, and that accordingly we should desire to understand alien scientific invention better, as we can already depend upon the unifying effect of feeling and instinct. It only remains to orient ourselves reasonably, both men and animals, by means of human thought.

All the ideas of all men are worthy of consideration and all can be useful to everyone in terms of the superior communal idea. There is no doubt that democracy, conceived as attainable truth, is a superior idea, the superior idea of man, seeing that it is the fundamental idea upon which man's complete life must be founded which our realist, Arcipreste de Hita, summed up in "getting a living and joyful intercourse." Progressive democracy is a state of perpetual transition toward universal aristocracy, which is the unanimous descent from everyone in everyone in a future of material and spiritual culture, and progressive democracy can not ever be considered (and today it is so considered) a progressive sickness of man, but rather a progressive immunization, seeing that all its elements should be health, strength, delicacy, grace, and beauty. Democracy will never be achieved as a characteristic of a particular people, a particular country as today they would like to consider it, but rather as common to all countries and their peoples. He who ought to be a democrat, a future aristocrat, is the common man and take note that "common" (all words contain in themselves, as do lives, their own absolute truth) signifies all that it should signify in this case. To arrive at the common democratic man it is necessary, without any animadversion, to be concerned with whatever is good in the ideology or sensitivity of all peoples. It is not possible to consider bad, or to condemn any ideological form in itself and in entirety, in cruel isolation, but only after friendly analysis in relation to other forms. We live by an equilibrium of analysis. I do not know whether all life is a deception, an illusion, but if it is we must maintain the illusion and the deception, which sustain us, in a way that suits all men without any part of them being obliged to become aware of it through difference in cultural level. Since unanimity of cultural levels is not now possible in all countries at the same time, we must approach each country on the same terms as those by which we live together in society in which we approach old people, youths, and children each at their own level. One of the major failings of our age is the disequilibrium between the three generations, sons, fathers, and grandfathers, which ought to be easy to resolve. We have to choose, we have to incorporate the best from each ideology, absolute or relative, and unite them progressively in a sheaf of the common superiority of reason.

Progress in democracy should consist in being sensitively concerned with the truest and most complete progress of democracy in all countries (at a determined moment of an epoch) and within all the favorable or adverse circumstances common to them, and in continuing to push against the obstacle, wherever it may be, without vanity or pride of race or country, to the point where it can be converted into the greatest possible good. The more of the future we may inject into the progressive present and the more we may keep of the progressive past, the more present quality we may obtain for ourselves and our contemporaries. It is interesting to realize that we are constantly concerned with the quality of so many minor things in our life: clothes, food, ornament, entertainment, etc., yet we do not take into account, or very much into account, the quality of superior, fundamental things. I have already pointed out in an earlier lecture that this is the fault of a progress disintegrated into a handful of nickels, a concern with abundance of sustenance. How we progress in candy-making, in the sweetness and texture of desserts, in the delicacy of bonbons and caramels, and how little in a greater and more universal human delicacy, the spiritual savor of life!

Progressive democracy, I believe, has to be based on and sustained by progressive love because love, too, has to feel itself as new, as an eternal present. So democracy as it moves onward will be ever new because its love is and will be ever new. I think of life as an eternal material and spiritual newness produced by continual love, everyday love, love which rises every day like the dawn. The complete man must be new, a child each day in all of his activities, major and minor (work, rest, sleep) if he wants them all to have this necessary quality by virtue of which he can leave them with pleasure and return to take them up again with pleasure. The awakening of a human being in despondency or joy ought to be a call to arms, a call to understand life in its entirety each day, our own life and that of others. I imagine all of humanity getting up each morning as an introduction to my daily life, taking from all of this what I should, and how useful to me is this exemplary preoccupation! To understand the daily lives of others and to share them with a tranquil, cultivated instinct, with a sympathy for what is constructive and what is unconstructive ought to be the norm common to all. With this feeling of loving, eternal, newness there should not appear to be anything old in the world, in the other sense of being useless, seeing that a spiritual, cultivated man, through the exaltation of his instinct can never be a superfluous, because dynamic idealism (even if it does not help a person already formed and physically decadent, in himself), can compensate for the lack of youthful, dynamic idealism and can be forever a new, dynamic idealism, and fully so, as in the beginning of autumn, thanks to their juices, the mature fruits of nature are always new.

In nature there are many things which, in order to become better, have to progress slowly, in logical evolution which is fundamentally true revolution and the authentic renewal. And the more completely progressive humanity is, the more it will be renewed because revolution expends its strength all at once and evolution is a permanent tonic. The greatest assassin of life is haste, the desire to reach things before the right time which means overreaching them. Simply by wishing for a quick sudden renewal humanity sometimes destroys itself for centuries.

And this happens because humanity, an organism with distinct organs, has to renew itself in all of them at whatever cost and, if not allowed to do so in the natural way in the proper rhythm and at the proper time, and when, because of continual obstacles, time and rhythm are altered, it attempts a solution by revolution instead, destroying the correct rhythm and the proper time and annihilating itself. And so nothing superior can be achieved in man as man achieves nothing superior in nature by altering the rhythm or timing of certain vegetables, minerals, or animals. What do I care about three annual crops of California apples, for example, which taste like wood, when I have another Spanish apple which takes a year to develop its juices? We can doubtless develop more numerous animals, fruits or minerals and those of greater size but what good are they? Only a satisfied, everyday hope in a better future, daily constancy and love, plus one's own work or that of others, can produce the complete fruit or the complete man.

A permanent state of transition is man's most noble condition. When we say an artist is in a state of transition, many believe that we are belittling. In my opinion when people speak of an art of transition this indicates a better art and the best that art can give. Transition is a complete present which unites the past and the future in a momentary progressive ecstasy, a progressive eternity, a true eternity of eternities, eternal moments. Progressive ecstasy is above all dynamic; movement is what sustains life and true death is nothing but lack of movement, be the corpse upright or supine. Without movement life is annihilated, within and without, for lack of dynamic cohesion. But the dynamism should be principally of the spirit, of the idea, it should be a moral dynamic ecstasy, dynamic in relation to progress, ecstatic in relation to permanence. Ecstasy ought to be the eternal definition of superior dynamism. The spirit always has defined the superior and life is beautiful and good when the superior remains defined as permanent movement.

Yes, I insist, we have to be concerned with life as dynamic ecstasy, as action in thought or feeling, and not as ecstatic dynamism for ecstatic dynamism would only be static spiritual movement. Dynamic ecstasy is absolute romanticism, absolute heroism. And here I return to my point. From my point of view, after the catastrophe which we feel and think is universal, a catastrophe resulting from an excess of useless dynamism, of useless progress, of useless realism, of useless technology, after this an attainable democracy is to be reached through the conception and realization of a new romanticism. I have referred various times to a North American friend of mine who believes that utopias are all realizable without losing the character of being eternal principles. A complete, normal romanticism could realize all that which up to now has been considered unrealizable. For years the poets, the artists, the scientists have gone on talking of a new romanticism. In the 18th and 19th centuries romanticism and democracy had a parallel existence (Shelley is the example); on the other hand they were separated by what is called romanticism, the false romanticism which abounded in the epoch (Byron for example), sustained by the concept of a false aristocracy, of life which failed to use romanticism as art. It seemed very beautiful to those who could enjoy a complete forgetfulness of the truly human but not to those generous and democratic spectators who were also false without knowing it, inferior to themselves, because they accepted the concept of democracy in a fatally inferior more or less revengeful sense. The romanticism of this epoch was an egoistic romanticism which means it was not romanticism. It was a poetic and political performance of useless heroism, out of proportion and melodramatic, a triumph, a vainglory, a boast which considered the world a round mirror of man's ignorance. When will the time come when men will be through with the idea of the world as a dramatic performance with parts for actors and parts for the audience? When will all men be real actors?

Will not our epoch be one of the establishment of the true romanticism? But we have to unite a divided world. In order to unite all in a universal drama (I do not know whether it will be a planetary theatrical performance but if it should be, it will have to be accepted and presented as the only truth possible to man today) in this drama we shall all participate equally, each taking an equal part, distributing the best and the worst equally, the agreeable and the disagreeable, all having an inherent feeling for beauty. Everything can be beautiful depending on the attitude with which it is approached. Sweeping does not appear beautiful from the point of view of getting rid of dirt with a broom, yet it can appear beautiful as rhythm and order and it certainly can appear so when considered as a divisible generous act of necessary cleanliness. And if life is drama thus it will be a beautiful and just drama in its inherent quality which results from a romanticism fused absolutely with the drama. The forge with a definite anvil. Democracy will beautify the drama of life if it is true democracy with heroic romanticism, sustained every day, hour, minute. The greatest gift that man can give and receive is love, who doubts it? And if love is not only individual but universal, its enjoyment will also be universal, it will be a unity of enjoyment. Progressive democracy would be something like the future of a joyous Christianity, without pomp, without struggle, without unnecessary martyrs, without purgatory, or hell, or heaven; the establishment of a vital paradise, a true existentialism, the complete comprehension of the sensitive ideology which man is capable of himself imagining and practising. The complete daily romanticism is a universal dream, dreamed and understood to the best of man's ability. The best example that man, great or poor, can give to the world in which he chances to live is, it seems to me, nothing more than superiority through universal and conscious love. And when he provides this example, not only other men of a group sympathetic to him but even the so-called inferior animals follow it.

A short time ago some young college students of Paraguay asked me whether the duty of the youth of the world was, at this moment of world history, to be combatant or spectator.

I answered them thus:

The world rotates in its orbit and its rotation goes forward in the only way it can go forward, in progress in the ideal. The rest is just wandering about, a wholesome gymnastic exercise. But every muscular rotation adds ideal force to increased physical force.

Today the most important of the so-called classes in our world because of the decisive fact of numbers is the people, and this anyone who cares to can see. The people, not taken into account for so many centuries by the two other isolated "classes," the so-called aristocracy and the so-called bourgeoisie.

Politics can push forward the evolution or the revolution of its country or even of other countries slightly but they alone create themselves. The human masses work like the terrestrial ones, their movements are similar, sometimes revolutionary (earthquakes, assassinations, lightning, etc.) and sometimes evolutionary. I believe that the youth of Paraguay, of Hispano-America, of all the world today, whether they wish it or not, are in this movement—evolutionary with constant probabilities of revolution. The important thing is to be conscious of it, to help it toward its aim, evolutionary whenever possible. In the case of extreme asphyxia, revolutionary. What other remedy remains? But it must be remembered that very often individual human revolutions happen without anything concrete being desired, the result of an electric phenomenon of our economic animal.

We must not forget the precept of the Inca, that good American, "If you raise your fist it means you have abandoned reason." And man differs from the geologic, with or without man, by virtue of reason.

Since the middle of the century we have been entering a new epoch of urgent dynamism, it is already a cliché to say so since we can all see it, too. It is not a question of ideas but of realities, of acts. Every day we hurry faster, whither it may be. The new epoch is forging itself in transcendental fires with a transcendental heroism. Man, youth above all, can help a little by means of heroic reason, in logical prose, not in fantastic verse, for poetry is the expression of peace. And heroic reason, firm, free in its unity, awaiting (Gandhi, for example, is the nearest to it) can be the best revolution, the most hygienic and convincing. I can not stop here to cite Gandhi without referring to a symposium of reminiscences that the review, *Sur*, of Buenos Aires has dedicated to him. It is gratifying that in a Hispano-American republic (in which I have the honor to reside temporarily) a homage has been rendered to the spirit represented by a man of another race and other circumstances, and it is lamentable to contrast this action of some conscious South Americans with that of some unconscious Europeans, for example, who summed up the death of Gandhi in disdain with the phrase "The struggle between the potgreens and the roastbeef is over."

The roastbeef and the potgreens, another class struggle. It seems to me that our duty as men journeying toward ourselves, toward our destiny, is to aid in the formation of a collective consciousness, both of those countries supposedly cultured and those supposedly uncultured, the consciousness of a world corresponding to the times as men conceive them.

Realidad, Buenos Aires/1948

WITH YOUR LIGHT

With your light you unite me to you, sun;
You unite all that shines to me,
By your light I am greater than all I see.

You are the only thing that draws me
Out of my inevitable atmosphere,
In whose depths,
As a fish in water, its inevitable water, I have to live
And I have to die
For you truly draw me out of my sight and my touch almost.
(Not as I draw myself out in a dream)
And you carry me, seeing and almost touching,
To shapes that are almost counterparts
Of my fish-dreams and my man-dreams.

You, sun, are the only thing
Which can console me with your littleness,
(A little larger than my shape)
For not being able to wholly abandon my depths.
I am the only thing
That shall be able to console you, sun,
With my inner greatness,
Greater than your inner greatness,
(If some day you can understand it)
For being no more than a star which shines on
Other people's dreams and carries them away.

You, sun, are not a god,
You are less god than I am god and man,
Because you do not know what you are, what god is, nor what
        I am,
And I know what and who you are and are not.

But you, sun, you carry me, you carry me, you carry me,
Rotating as I rotate and you rotate,
Sun, with your coal, your flaming ember,
You carry me
To a more real distance than any god or man.

Una colina meridiana/1942-1950

ITS CORONET OF GLORY

Under the elm tree
All the leaves are lying.
It looks at them, fallen,
They see the blue glory
With a white cloud
That is now its coronet.
Up there they were all
Laughing with the birds.
(Today the grey squirrels
Jump madly between them.)

I do not burn the leaves, I let them
Pleasantly enter
The earth which always
Nourishes their mouths
So that the roots may
Grant them their red souls,
The roots which have been
The profound shapers.

Would that none might be lost,
Not one, not one!

238

Would that once again
They might all be green singers.
Would that all might return
To the glory of its coronet,
Would that all might possess
Their glory in its coronet!

Una colina meridiana/1942-1950

FROM LOWER TAKHOMA
STANZAS OF THE THREE LOST ONES

(to Idea)
Of the first:
THE PAIR

Lonely falcon lifting
The twins of your separated
Shadow,
Your fixed cry names you.

Your separate twins,
My shadow more than my shadow.
Separated.
My tall cry names you.

Because I, too, would fly,
Fly, your shadow is my shadow.
Separated.
Your sharp cry names me.

Falcon, I, a man, lift
The twins of my separated

Shadow,
My wide cry names me.

Of the third:
THIS SOLITUDE

The yellow solitude
Offers me one color only.
Only. A color.
       Or death.

Is not solitude my life?
The yellow was my strength!
"Your solitude . . . you know it well."
Only? A color?
       Or death?

May the yellow say to me,
"Your color? . . . here you have it!"
A color. Only.
       Or death.

Only with the forevermine,
Only with the mineforever
(For the two are both alone.)
Only. A color.
       I. And death.

Of the second:
THEREFORE NEVER

The sun strikes in another way
On this strange hillside

Which does not end.
Therefore I am strange.

Because this unusual roadway
Was my absurd destiny
Which does not end.
Therefore I alone go.

Because in me, the mistaken one,
All is shadow of that other side
Which does not end.
Therefore I am always other.

Because I go out of this life
With its unknown land
Which does not end.
Therefore never is my today.

Una colina meridiana/1942-1950

WITH HER AND WITH THE CARDINAL

You have seen them, those elm trees
On the slope of yonder hillside
Setting fire to their time
With their own red and endless light,
Those elmtrees, when we turned back at night
To look at them, red in their places,
Were dreaming that they burned in the eyes
Of the ones who discovered them in their corner.

What a fire that was, what elm trees were there
For us,
Were there just for us alone, in a place
That one longs to come back to see, come back to see,
Always come back to see the same thing!

No, it was not wandering gold in constant gold,
It was gold in action, it was gold in an orbit,
It was a star of gold in a red tree,
With spaces of earth among its branches
With a cardinal of glory
Withdrawn among mute, folded wings,
Spaces no longer of sky
But of inner eternity.

You have seen them, those elm trees.
Do not tell me again they were not the ones,
The ones we dreamed of.
They were the ones,
The ones on the slope of yonder hillside,
Setting fire to their time, the lofty time,
With their own red and endless light.

Una colina meridiana/1942-1950

IN MY THIRD SEA

You were in my third sea,
You, that color of all colors

(As one day I described your whiteness),
That sound of all sounds
That I followed forever with the color
Through air, earth, water, fire, and love,
Past the grey terminal of all departures.

You were, you came to be, you are the love
In fire, water, earth, and air,
Love in my man's body and in woman's body,
Love which is the form,
Unique and complete,
Of the natural element which is the element
Of everything, the element forever;
And I have had you and shall have you forever
Except that not all see you,
Except that we who look at you do not see you until a certain
    day.

The most complete love, love, this you are,
With all the substance
(And with all the essence)
In all the senses of my body
(And in all the sense of my soul)
Which are the same in the great knowledge
Which anyone, as I do now, knows wholly, in light.

I know it for I knew it more and more;
The more, the more, the only road to knowledge;
Now I know and I am complete
Because you, my longed-for god, are visible,
Are audible, are perceptible
In the murmur and the color of the sea, now,

243

Because you are the mirror of myself
In the world, greater through you, who have touched me.

Animal de fondo/1949

WITHOUT TEDIUM OR REST

If I have gone out so much in the world
It has been only and always
To meet you, longed-for god,
Among so much head and so much breast
Of so many men.

(Gigantic city, great concourse,
Which returns to me in a gray reflection of water,
In this blue sun in a south full of light,
Of this longed-for and longing god,
Eyes, and eyes, and eyes,
With sparkling instantaneous movements
Of the eternal in motion.)

So much mover of thought and feeling,
(Black, white, yellow, red, green
In body) with the soul
Drifting toward you,
Becoming itself,
Happening in me,
Without knowing it, or I or they knowing it!

Universal design, in flames
Of shadows and inquiring
And hoping lights,
Of an immense observing eye which spies you out
With the pain or joy
Of a restless, adventurous, wandering.
And I, in the midst, possessor now,
Of your consciousness, god, through awaiting you
From my destined childhood,
Without rest or tedium.

Animal de fondo/1949

WITH THE SOUTHERN CROSS

The southern cross is projected upon a cloud
And looks at me with diamond eyes,
My eyes more profound than love,
With a love forever known.

It was, it was, it was
In all of the blue sky of my immanence;
Its four eyes were pure consciousness,
The progressive solution of a beauty
Which was awaiting me in the kite
Still, that I was flying when a child.

I have arrived, I have arrived
At my penultimate day of illusion

Of the conscious god of myself and mine,
At kissing its eyes, its stars
With the four kisses of living love;
The first on the eyes of its forehead,
The second, the third, on the eyes of its hands,
And the fourth on the eye of its foot, that of a lofty mermaid.

The southern cross is watching over me,
Over my ultimate innocence,
Over my return to the child-god which I was one day
In my Moguer of Spain.

And below, far below me, in the loftiest earth,
Which leads to my most precise profundity,
A warm mother nourishes me with a silent mouth
As she nourished me in her living lap
When I flew my white kites,
And now with me she feels all the stars
Of the round, full, eternity of night.

Animal de fondo/1949

IN THE BEST THAT I HAVE

Green sea and grey sky and blue sky
And loving albatrosses in the wave,
And in everything, the sun, and you in the sun, watching,
Longed-for and longing god,
Lighting my arrival with different golds,

The arrival of *this* which I am now,
Of *this* which even yesterday I doubted
Whether I could be, in you, as I am.

What a transformation of the man in me, longing god,
From being doubtful of the legend
Of the god so many spoke of,
To being a firm believer
In the history that I myself have created
From all of my life for you!

Now I come to this termination
Of a year of my natural life,
In the surrounding air in which I possess you,
Summit of this sea, in surrounding water,
This beautiful, blind frontier
Through which you are entering me,
Content to be yours and to be mine
In the best that I have, all I express.

Animal de fondo / 1949

WITH HALF OF ME YONDER

My silver here in the south, in this south,
Consciousness in shining silver, palpitating
In the clean morning,
When the springtime draws flowers from my inmost self!

My silver, here, response of the silver
That dreamed this silver in the clean morning
Of my Moguer of silver,
Of my Puerto of silver,
Of my Cádiz of silver,
I a sad child always dreaming
Of the beyond-the-sea with the beyond-the-earth, the beyond-the-
sky.

And the beyond-the-sky was here
With this earth, the beyond-the-earth,
This beyond-the-sea, with this sea;
And here in this beyond-the-sea, my manhood found
Its complete consciousness, in the north and the south,
Because this was lacking.

And I am joyful now with a fulfilled joy,
With half of me yonder, my yonder, completing me,
For I now possess my completion,
My silver here in the south, in this south.

Animal de fondo / 1949

LOOKING AT HER HANDS

In light or in shade, the background scarcely seen, (this golden
dark, this cold clarity) these human hands at work, the right
hand which undertakes everything, the left which assists it,

understanding it, giving the light touch which completes, these hands are the most clearly deciphered key to him who contemplates his own destiny (and the other destiny which is the other and more his own).

Working hands which obey instinct and intelligence, free of a pervasive consciousness which oversees them, to which they are like daughters of a god and the active part, but which they never see because they are closed. (And sometimes, how often, they obey the thoughts and emotions of others, creating with their already invisible image, the unattainable.)

Friend, always look at working hands. Look at these familiar feminine hands, the right aided by the left (so small, all soul and steel), look at the sensitive hand, the thoughtful hand. See how they grasp and let go, how they fold themselves and turn, how they caress, how they reach up, how bravely they attack, how gently! And then see them with a book, beneath it yet so skilfully placed, peacefully accompanying the reading matter.

(The right hand which I squeeze, a left that I kiss.) Think, friend . . . of dead hands, at rest but no longer hands, with their history beneath them, too, like a breast grown cold! And what a history (and perhaps what a legend, then) the stillness of certain hands, one day, of these hands.

Ríos que se van/1951-1953

THE COLOR OF YOUR SOUL

While I am kissing you, the murmur
Creates the tree for us as it rocks

Gold in the sun, gold the sun grants as it flies,
Ephemeral treasure of the tree, the tree of my love.

It is not radiance, or ardor, or loftiness
Which gives me all of you that I adore
In the waning light, it is the gold, the gold,
It is the gold made into shadow, your color.

The color of your soul, for your eyes
Are turning into it, and in the same measure
As the sun exchanges its golds for reds
And you are left melted and dim,
The gold pours forth, made you, from your two eyes
Which are my peace, my faith, my sun, my life!

Ríos que se van / 1951-1953

TO BURN COMPLETELY

Our happiness, it seems to me, consists of making good use of
the time and space in which our destiny confines us for if it is
true that we are faced with them here through no choice of
our own, it is also true that we have been brought here endowed
with an instinct which, by means of our education and culture,
we can transform into a superior insight, and I do not mean a
superior intelligence because, for me, the intelligence is in no
way superior to the instinct which is all eyes, and blind intelli-
gence turned outward can not serve to guide a man through his
environment but can only help him to understand it. In this

manner, from our first moment of life, our invulnerable inno-
cence has been able to confront us with the adventure and we
are rich in inner and outer weapons which contain, from the
spontaneous to the conscious and vice versa, all the potentiali-
ties for progress in truth, beauty, and love.

And our continual progress has to contribute to our happiness
because, if progress does not promote human happiness, what
good is it? The true man, the authentic man, the inherent culti-
vated aristocrat, who unites the greatest sensitivity in daily life
to the greatest richness of a greater life, is he who most desires
the happiness of the world, he who seeks his own happiness in
universal happiness, he who succeeds, by means of a clear con-
cept of the whole life of the world, in best occupying, using, and
enjoying his space and time.

To be man at his best, the complete *aristo,* is the goal of every
man. If a man does not orient himself in the world toward his
goal, he lives provisionally and to live provisionally is not the
destiny of life, it is not really living. In this world we have to
burn completely, resolve ourselves fully, each one in the flames
and the resolution appropriate to him. For no creator or created
god would accept those who have not wholly fulfilled life, life
as a whole, and certainly not the limited life that Calderon posits
in his nonsensical, *The Great Theater of the World.* Let us not
forget that Jesus of Nazareth (for this was his name, not Christ)
in the rapid tragedy of his life, supreme aristocrat that he was,
pardoned the Magdalene, now a saint, because she had loved
much and Dimas because he had loved quickly, and Mary of
Magdalene and Dimas, who merited Jesus' most beautiful
words, "Tonight ye shall be with me in Paradise," were certainly
saved by having burned generously in different flames. Today
perhaps we would have taken the Magdalene to a psychiatrist
who would have put her in a grim hospital which certainly
would not have been heaven but. . . . Progress with a capital
letter; and for greater security they would have hanged Dimas. We

who live as if in a boarding school, a boarding school of air, lit with the coals of a red hot sun, like ours, and with the hope of rewards or punishments elsewhere, lose a secure existence and another probable or attainable one because each life must maintain a unity from beginning to end.

Our life is a beginning and an end with no more than a brief, progressive contact with its boundaries and, since we remember nothing concrete before the beginning, we have to treat it always and solely as an end, even if it be not, and we ought to convince all other people that they should treat it the same way. We can depend much more on reaching an end than on coming from a beginning. When we all come to treat our existence as end, we shall all find a satisfying paradise in it; this is a personal preoccupation which does not evade collective morality (I am not he), an attainable belief in other made to order paradises, which shall be our concern when they come to us, if they do come to us, since they are things that must come to us, like our parents, and we do not go to them (the imagination is autonomous and I am an imaginative autonomist). It is just as when we concern ourselves with a trip to the Arctic or to Ecuador on our own planet, places which become these places with these names only when we see them, not while we imagine them.

Almost all transitory religions have been invented in this world as a remote consolation for the poor, the sick, or the disinherited morally and physically. "When I am sick" said Yeats, the true Irish poet, always master of beauty, "I think of God, when I am well I go to the beach to play ball with the fairies." To accept religion as a collective ideal, when one has not yet determined one's own ideals, is good, no one doubts it, above all in early youth and better yet in adolescence, but when we are fully mature we can also aspire, or aspire in addition, to personal ideals, personal religions, science, poetry, art, all of which are not necessarily a consolation for inadequacies or a desire for particular things but are the roots of our wings, peace, and enjoyment, vocations founded on the most immediate concept of beauty and truth, intimate vocations which are genuinely idealistic, that is to say, a concept more human and also more divine since, by fulfilling our vocation, we are realizing God in truth and beauty.

We need never regard the ideal as distant or non-existent because the ideal is in ourselves. What I mean is we should not place the ideal at heights marked by an elevator which always goes down, as do certain poets of the fifth floor or the cellar, these extremes being their maximum heights and depths, but that we possess proof that we can extract the ideal from any form which exists. God is not only in the cooking pots of St. Teresa, or in the plow, or in the forge, or in the oar, but also in the lyre, in the pen, the microscope, the brush, the musical note, etc. A realistic being does not, as a logical consequence have to be a non-idealistic being and existentialism can roll itself in dung but likewise bathe in the sea. The poet knows that he does not reach his ideal which is to say he does not kill it which is to say that he ought not to reach it by killing it, but this by no means indicates that he should consider it unattainable. On the contrary, the unattainable and non-existent is what is killed, what has been killed, because poetry is precisely a divine art and divine signifies original, fundamental; poetry is making divine what we have at hand, the beings and the things which we have the good fortune to possess, not as ideals to be pursued but as substances which contain essences. Yes, I maintain that the ideal exists and that it is close by if we admit that since it is ours it is of our essence and our substance. We are made of the ideal and by virtue of this we can all find it in everyone, seeing that we are all treasurers of consciousness. Our only problem is to find it and to understand the significance of the verb to find; it is life itself and all the lives that may come to us beyond the origin of death. I believe that the ideal could consist in making life ideal, exalting us while creating standards for us, stand-

ards and ideals for all lives, by exalting them, for man possesses
the faculty of creating and contemplating, of mixing work and
leisure, profound leisure and profound work. If we promote as-
piration toward the ideal in others, we shall be much closer to
realizing it, once others can see it thus, in ourselves. To create
an ideal does not mean to stop taking part in daily life, in the
communal, as it is popularly believed; the ideal orients life
between angel and demon in a spasm of simultaneous mutual
liberty and unity at the point of contact which separates and
unites at the same time, although admittedly it wounds, man
and woman each possessing a white wing and a black wing. I
insist we have to find the ideal, to find the center of our lives, the
diamond in the ore, and to find this incubator which is the ore
we must first feel ecstasy for it, like the poet, in order to under-
stand it and then more dynamically to love it and enjoy it, to
recreate it every day in every sense of the word, recreate and
likewise recreate confidence in it and of it every day, which is the
only way to realize it wholly and progressively by consuming it,
the only way to continue to be worthy of our consciousness, our
longed-for and longing God.

When we contemplate things and beings, when we love them
and enjoy them, when we have their confidence, having given
them ours; when we concern ourselves with them through our
complete consciousness and, as complete consciousness, they
manifest their content to us, we shall possess their most pro-
found secrets and thus they will be able to offer themselves to us
as an ideal, for perhaps the ideal may be a secret of which only
the most loving are worthy. It is difficult for a man to conceive
himself living a life with more elements of happiness than this
life we are living, a life doubtless like others past or to come, for
what a man imagines can not be more than inner imagery, or a
more or less beautiful modification of what is outside him, of
what he feels with his bodily and spiritual five senses, since there
is nothing more filled with spirit than the senses. I never forget

that when my mother felt a pain in her temples, the most delicate surface of the body, she said that her sense hurt her. Our duty, desire, and ability must be none other than to conceive and orient our life to the best of our ability as a unique and definitive perhaps. And I do not mean by this that we must be pessimistic, since fantasy is also a characteristic of man and to fantasy is to realize dreams by means of the will. A fantasy can be equivalent to a paradise and if the fantasy passes, better yet, because eternal paradise would be very boring and indeed those fakirs who resolve themselves in an unconscious nirvana, in a death without worms, anticipate this boredom.

Real life is reality with fantasy; to better conceive and orient our real life implies that we have invented this entelechy which we call progress, "The progression of consciousness which conceives, orients, and controls life."

Centro, Buenos Aires/1956

8

Thirty selections from the many aphorisms written throughout Jiménez's life

1

My interior life, eternal beauty, my Work.

2

Classic is all which having been (or rather, by having been) exact in its time, is transcendent, enduring.

3

Not a day . . . without destroying a page.

4

You find in solitude only what you take to it.

5

What a conflict within me between my good and my best!

6

To encourage the young, to be exigent with, to chastise the mature, to tolerate the old.

7

With beauty you have to live (and die) alone.

8

I keep Poetry hidden in my house like a beautiful woman for her pleasure and mine, and our relationship is that of passionate lovers.

9

Dynamism, drunkenness, grace, glory . . . my Poetry!

10

Purify: recreate.

11

The true sign of poetry is contagion; this does not mean (take care!) imitation.

12

Style is not the pen . . . or language.

13

If anyone seeks me in this life (and in death) let him look only in beauty.

14

What youth thinks of us is very important for youth is the beginning of our posterity.

15

My best work is my constant repentance for my work.

16

My soul, mirror in darkness, wherever you may be you catch the light.

17

Let us cultivate, above all, the will to reject.

18

Criticism: I do not tolerate condescension and I demand justice.

19

Roots and wings—but let the wings take root and the roots fly.

20

For my part, in life (or in death) there are no reasons but esthetic reasons.

21

The world does not grow old, it is rejuvenated with the centuries.

22

In the provisional, exactitude, too, as if it were definitive.

23

Let us seek the great joy of having done.

24

To be brief is the supreme morality of art.

25

To keep it all—but with effort.

26

On land the swan is a goose.

27

Sad flower, opened by force!

28

Imperfection, like precision, is not sought, we hit upon it, (or is it grace?).

29

To correct: to arrange surprise.

30

The poem should be like a star which is a world and looks like a diamond.